MW01065349

EXPOSED

TRUE STORIES OF MESSY SURVIVALS
FROM ROLLA, MO

Published in Beaverton, Oregon, by Good Catch Publishing.
www.goodcatchpublishing.com
V1.1

Printed in the United States of America

TABLE OF CONTENTS

DEDICATION

For those who are tired and looking for true rest —
we offer our love and support.

ACKNOWLEDGEMENTS

I would like to thank Eddie Jones for his vision for this book and Anita Agers-Brooks for her hard work in making it a reality. To the people of CLC, thank you for your boldness and vulnerability in sharing your personal stories.

This book would not have been published without the amazing efforts of our project manager and editor, Holly De Herrera. Her untiring resolve pushed this project forward and turned it into a stunning victory. Thank you for your great fortitude and diligence. Deep thanks to our incredible editor in chief, Michelle Cuthrell, and executive editor, Jen Genovesi, for all the amazing work they do. I would also like to thank our invaluable proofreader, Melody Davis, for the focus and energy she puts into perfecting our words.

Lastly, I want to extend our gratitude to the creative and very talented Ariana Randle, who designed the beautiful cover for *Exposed: True Stories of Messy Survivals from Rolla, MO.*

Daren Lindley
President and CEO
Good Catch Publishing

The book you are about to read
is a compilation of authentic life stories.
The facts are true, and the events are real.
These storytellers have dealt with crisis, tragedy, abuse
and neglect and have shared their most private moments,
mess-ups and hang-ups in order for others to learn and
grow from them. In order to protect the identities of those
involved in their pasts, the names and details of some
storytellers have been withheld or changed.

INTRODUCTION

Have you ever had a secret you didn't want anyone to know about? Most of us have. Have you ever feared others might unearth your secret, causing you humiliation and possibly costing you everything? You're not alone. Have you battled depression and anxiety so thick, it made you feel like you might suffocate? These are real issues suffered by many.

It's lonely struggling through painful events without support. The weight is heavy when we attempt to carry our burdens in private. Our emotions can smother all attempts at happiness.

We don't keep secrets — secrets keep us.

But there is another way.

Discover death-defying, astounding and hope-filled people whose gripping stories offer the rest of us inspiration. Sometimes survival is messy, and support arrives from surprising or unexpected places.

Walk with real people who faced real pain in real ways. Their pasts did not define them. They learned it's never too late for a fresh start. May their stories inspire the rest of us to break free of our secrets, too.

I GOT THIS
THE STORY OF DAVID
WRITTEN BY ALEXINE GARCIA

I held my lighter in my lap, ready to pull it apart. Hidden inside, next to the fluid, was a small bag of meth. I was driving to my favorite spot and anxious to get the stuff in my system. I looked around and then in my rearview mirror.

That's when I spotted him. Two cars back was the same black car I'd seen in my neighborhood. *Tailing me? Snooping? Was it an unmarked police car?* I turned left at the stoplight, and the black car turned left. *But what if I'm wrong? What if I'm just being paranoid?* I didn't use my blinkers and made a sudden right turn at a side street. The black car jerked and made an awkward turn as well.

I got angry. Almost certain it was the same car, I had to be sure. I turned in at the grocery store and circled the lot. Sure enough, the other car followed me. My buddy had warned me, but I didn't believe him.

Looks like he was right. The feds are onto me.

శశశ

The cool guys I wanted to hang out with just stood in the corner of a church parking lot. I looked around to make sure no one was watching, and I reached down into the center of the pine tree. My hand felt around for my box of cigarettes. I jammed them into my pocket, got back onto my bike and rode over to the older group of boys. My heart beat fast with nervousness. I pulled out my pack.

"You guys got a light?" I asked, flashing my box.

They laughed and looked at each other. "Yeah, I got a Zippo, but I also got something better than that."

My hands got clammy. If I smoked with these guys, I was sure to be in the "in" crowd. If I smoked weed with them, then I'd really be set up.

"Oh, really?" I said with a smirk. Before I knew it, they passed their joint my way. I was into cigarettes so I didn't even cough. This became a weekly thing. Whenever I passed by on my bike, they'd wave me over. We passed around joints in the church parking lot and rode our bikes around the block.

One day the kids were all out of weed, so we rode our bikes over to some guy's house. The lawn was overgrown, and bikes littered the front patio. James didn't even knock before he opened the door. He looked back at me and said, "We come here a lot."

We walked into a smoke-filled living room with Led Zeppelin blaring. Kids from my high school were sitting on the couch or on the floor passing bongs and joints around and playing cards.

"Who's this guy?" An older man sitting in a recliner pointed his chin at me.

"Oh, this is David. We met him at the First Baptist parking lot a few weeks ago. He's safe," James said.

I GOT THIS

Someone handed him a joint. He took a long draw, then held his breath for a few seconds before letting it out. "We came to get a dime." They exchanged money and a baggy. All the while, the older guy, Dan, kept his eyes on me.

"What's your story, David?"

"Uh, I dunno. I go to high school," I said. His constant eye on me was unnerving. "I play sports."

"Oh, okay. Come in, have a seat. Make yourself at home." By this point my friends were already sitting with bongs or cards in hand.

I noticed kids around the glass coffee table cutting lines of coke. I'd never seen it before, but I had sense enough to know what it was. Dan watched me closely.

"You want to give it a try?" He grinned, nonchalant.

"I don't know," I said, staring all the while at the guy with long hair snorting a line.

"Just give it a try. You'll love it."

A girl with a pretty smile made me a small skinny line and showed me how to inhale it with a straw. And I did love it. It made my chest swell up with courage. I felt completely alert and full of happiness. The whole bike ride home, I pedaled hard, letting the wind rush through me. I didn't stop at stop signs to look both ways. Cars stopped for me. I felt invincible.

Whenever we went back to Dan's house, I felt so cool. Only certain kids were allowed at his house. We were the in crowd, the elite. A few months after my first hit of coke, I started thinking, *If I bought an eight ball, I'd get a gram for free.* I could get by on the gram and sell the eight ball to my friends at school. I hung around with the jocks, but I knew well enough who smoked and who did coke.

Sure enough, I was right. I didn't have to pay for my drugs after that. I had weed and coke whenever I wanted. I hid my drug use from my parents. As far as they knew, I was a good kid, one of the top athletes at school, earning A's in class. Or that's what my parents bragged to their friends.

I came from a good family. My parents never divorced, they didn't abuse me and we weren't poor. There was no real reason for me to get into drugs. It was just a choice I made.

I continued to use even after I graduated high school. Instead of attending college, I went straight to work, wherever I could find a job. My main concern was pretty much getting high.

సాసాస

When I was 24, my family and I watched my dad deteriorate. The cancer in his lymph nodes grew an inch a day, and the light slowly drained right out of his eyes. He'd been in remission for eight years, and we'd stopped fearing the cancer might return. When Dad retired, my parents moved to Missouri, where my dad spent his last years hunting and fishing. But when the cancer came back, it came back strong. I flew from California often to be with him. He had peace, but that didn't make things any easier for me.

I GOT THIS

When he passed away, people tried to comfort my family at the funeral.

"God had a bigger plan for your dad's life," one woman said. *How the heck do you know that?* I thought, glaring at her. I was so mad at God.

I didn't believe in him, but I was also mad at him.

Growing up, I often put God to the test by asking him, "If you are really real, make that limb fall from the tree. If you're real, show me something real." I needed something concrete, physical. If I couldn't touch it or see it, it wasn't real to me.

I often wondered, *If you are such a caring God, why would you let innocent babies die?* God was just a selfish jerk.

When my dad died, I decided that God was a senseless, selfish SOB. How could Charles Manson be alive in prison while my dad died in the hospital? My anger surfaced in everything I did. I was rude to people, and I wore a constant scowl.

The following year, I met my first wife. My neighbor was dating her friend, and the four of us started going out together. Lauren and I moved to Missouri together and got married. I worked driving trucks for a while, then did some masonry work.

Then I started working for a telephone wiring company. It was rigorous manual labor that paid really well. We installed major wiring systems at hospitals, military bases and smaller offices as well. The company was commissioned to create the largest system we had ever manufactured to be sent over to Saudi Arabia during the Gulf War. We were only given 16 days to complete the project, and we had never built anything in under 30 days. The work team consisted of two shifts of five members each. We worked 20-hour days and went back to our hotel rooms to sleep for four hours.

The cycle wore us down, and by the 12th day, the majority of us were lying out on the boxes. We could hardly talk without slurring, much less think. Serious sleep deprivation had set in. We were spent, but not Vince. He just continued to work, tying down cables and screwing wires.

"How in the world are you still at it?" I asked him.

"Let me show you." He showed us his tiny baggy of meth, and he even shared with all of us. It was similar to coke, but almost better. I felt more than invincible. I felt like I could conquer the world, that I could stop bullets. We got the project done in 15 days.

We felt quite accomplished as we watched our work get loaded onto the huge cargo plane. It got even better when we were given a $1,500 bonus and certificates from the military. I sure was flying high. There wasn't much I felt I couldn't accomplish.

My promotion to project manager only boosted my ambitions. I carried this winning streak into my personal life and started selling drugs again, like when I was a kid. But this time I upped my game by selling larger amounts.

I worked hard for days at a time and then my body would crash. I'd sleep for several days in a row. I didn't care if I missed work. My looks deteriorated. My house was a mess, and it all didn't matter as long as I was getting my high and my sleep.

"David, I don't know how to tell you this, but we need you to bring in the van. It's over."

"What do you mean? And why are you firing me over the phone? This just isn't right."

"I can't fire you in person because you hardly show up. The guys told me about all the service calls you've missed. I'm sorry. You used to do so well. I don't know what has happened to you over the last few months."

I knew good and well, but I didn't want to face it. In the beginning, I was getting it all done. I worked 12 to 15 hours at a time. But the more I tweaked, the fuzzier my brain got. I started just running around trying to do seven things at once, but none of it really got finished.

I knew the telephone company well, so I started my own business. It was easy for me to pick up several contracts and hire on employees.

My life became a routine of cycles. There was the wake and sleep cycle. I did meth or coke or both in the morning to wake up from coming down off the drugs. All day I worked, pushed drugs, smoked weed, partied or whatever else was on the agenda for that day. My body collapsed at the end of the day, and the next day I woke up, snorted some coke or meth or both and did it all again.

Then there was the smuggling routine. My buddies and I packed up $145,000 in Saran Wrap, covered it in axle grease, more Saran Wrap, more axle grease, more

Saran Wrap, then duct tape. We couldn't have the dogs smelling the money or the drugs on the money. We took apart the dash of a rental car and inserted the package. Then a hired "mule" drove the rental down to Mexico and drove back with a brick of meth. The car came in, and we pulled apart the dash or the door and unwrapped the package. It was 10 pounds of meth. We inserted a new axle-greased, plastic-wrapped package, and the cycle started over.

Then there was the work cycle. I woke up, did my drugs, flew to whatever city I had a contract with. I did my work, hit up the local bars, smoked, snorted, went to bed, flew home and then started up again a few days later.

I met Becky while on one of those trips.

She was into the same kind of fun I was, and we had chemistry right away. I didn't have to hide my infatuation with coke, meth and money from her because we were on the same page.

A few months later, I told my wife that things weren't working out. Lauren did not like coke and meth. I had to hide my addictions and my illegal activities from my two daughters. The double life wore me thin. I had to choose, and I chose the drugs.

My mother and siblings were onto me, too. There I was, thinking I was doing so well hiding the drugs, but it was written all over my face. My skin took on a waxy gray tint, and I grew thin. Dark bags hung under my eyes.

"You don't come to our family barbeques anymore," my mom said.

I GOT THIS

"Why do you bother even showing up?" my sis said. "You show up late, hardly eat, then leave early."

I knew they were right. The only person I was lying to was myself. I thought I lived this double life, playing the family businessman by day, drug-pushing addict at night, but everyone could see that the two met right in the middle. I lived in a small town, and people whispered behind my back.

About this time, a buddy tipped me off. He told me the feds were onto me. Of course, I thought I could outsmart them. I saw their unmarked cars parked around my neighborhood. One evening I was driving away from home to smoke meth when I saw one of them following me. Of course, I wasn't certain, so I pulled into a grocery store parking lot and took a few turns and figured out that they were in fact following me. Somehow I was able to outrun them that night.

Then Lyle, who was in the pushing business with me, asked me to come look at his phone. I came over with my tool bag and unscrewed his phone from the wall. The tiny wire that connected the phone to the wall was missing. I got the chills realizing what I was looking at.

"Take a look at this, Lyle," I said.

He peered around inside the panel and said, "What am I looking at? You're the expert, David."

"There's a small cord missing. These things don't just turn up missing on their own."

He realized that someone had been in his house messing with his phone.

EXPOSED

I went back home and hooked a voltmeter to my phone and had Lyle call me. The volts went down when I answered, then dropped again when we started talking, which indicated there was a recording device hooked up to the line.

These guys must have overlooked the fact that I was in the telephone business. So we simply took all the wire out of our houses and replaced it with AC wire. This fried their recording devices. We also moved our conversations to pre-paid cell phones.

I upped my game at this point. I never brought dope into the house. I created secret compartments inside my flowerpots and hid stashes in them. If I carried large quantities, it was always in the motor compartment or under the chassis of the vehicle. My personal goods were hidden in the inside of a lighter and then nonchalantly thrown on the floorboard of the car.

The constant spinning in circles gradually wore me down. I smoked my meth out of a glass pipe and watched the thick white smoke make tendrils in the air. *I've got to change my life around,* I thought. It was just that, though. A thought. It really wasn't something I knew how to act on at that point. Everything was so out of control, I wouldn't even have known where to start.

"Dad, we want you around for a long time, you know," Kara said over the phone. It was another one of her sessions lecturing me. I never imagined that my 20-year-old kid would be lecturing me someday. But that was the case. "I know you don't like to hear it, but you need God in your life. Will you please come to church with Ron and the kids and me?"

I couldn't even fathom the thought of it. I knew she was right about me straightening my life out. I was tired of hiding. I was tired of getting high and crashing. I just didn't see any way of ending it.

Her insisting turned to begging. Every Friday night she called and invited me to the Sunday service. I finally cracked and said yes simply because I thought it would get her off my back.

"Wait, what? Did you just say yes?"

I chuckled. "Surprised, aren't you?"

"You've only turned me down a couple hundred times."

Agreeing to go to church and going to church were two different animals. As soon as we pulled into the parking lot, my stomach tightened with nervousness. I had an actual physical reaction to it. We walked through the lobby, and one person after another greeted Kara. I felt like an outsider. People gathered in their little cliques, and Kara flowed between each of them, with me hovering by her side. I wore a fake smile as she introduced me to one person after another. I was screaming on the inside as pools of sweat gathered at my armpits. I was glad for the jacket I wore.

I don't know why but I joined her the following Sunday. The third week, I realized that it was the friendly people who kept me coming back. Her friends and the people who sat in the same row as us remembered my name. As I came back repeated times, I saw that these people actually acted like the sermons told them to. Their smiles were real. They asked about my week and actually cared. It got weirder when I started reading the Bible on my own. *Jesus hung around people just like me,* I realized. His disciples doubted him. He talked to an adulteress.

"You're a mess, but I'm a mess, too," the pastor said from the pulpit. This was new to me. "The only perfect person the world has ever seen was Jesus. I have a bit of news for you all — there are no perfect people here! If you came here to sit amongst perfect people, you're in the wrong church."

I felt like this man was talking right to me. It went on like that for weeks. His words struck a chord with everything I was thinking.

Easter was only a few weeks away, and Pastor Eddie was preaching about Jesus on the cross. Those sorts of things never made sense to me before. God was nothing but a selfish being, and Christians were hypocrites. That's what I'd thought for years. But all of that was what I observed from a distance. There, up close, I saw the fallacies in my beliefs. Pastor Eddie explained that God gave up his son, Jesus. That got my attention. *How could a selfish God give up his own son to save people?*

"Jesus died on the cross to pay the price for your sins." *How could a selfish God die such a gruesome death when he was not at fault?* "You don't have to pass some ridiculous test. You don't need to jump through hoops to get to heaven. What you need to do is confess your sins to

God and believe that Jesus was raised on the third day and that he lives today."

Was it that easy? I could ask God for his forgiveness and he would give it to me? I looked around at all the people I had grown to know over the past months. Their eyes were fixed on Pastor Eddie. They believed. They were not "good" people. They were once sitting in my spot, asking themselves these same questions.

"If you want to have this forgiveness for yourself, if you want to believe it is a free gift, I want to invite you up here to the pulpit to pray for salvation today." The band played soft music, while people stood and walked to the front of the church. I stood and joined them. I walked to the pulpit, and I felt perfectly comfortable about it. I didn't feel out of my realm or judged. This was exactly what I needed. Pastor Eddie told us to pray with him, so I bowed my head and repeated the prayer after him.

"God, please forgive me for my sins. I need you so badly in my life. I believe that your son, Jesus Christ, died on the cross for my sins. He rose on the third day, and I want him to live in me. I want to accept him as Savior and Lord of my life."

I didn't have one of those emotional church moments of tears and overwhelming joy. But I did believe that it was all true. A feeling of peace came over me. My future looked extremely uncertain, but all that mattered to me in that moment was that new and wonderful sense of peace.

I became a parking lot volunteer. My job was to wave to people and direct them to open parking spots. It didn't seem like much, but oftentimes the parking lot volunteers were the first smiling faces that people saw at church. Sometimes people came speeding into the lot, and we had to keep our cool and remain understanding.

"Hello, folks. Welcome to Christian Life Center," I said to an elderly couple as they arrived one Sunday. The gentleman helped his wife out of the car and came over to me.

"Good morning," he said. "You know, we were heading to another church up the street, but I saw you there smiling and waving, and I just felt compelled to come here. Thank you so much."

"Thank you, sir." Those were the kind of incidents that made me realize what being part of a church was all about. Serving God meant reaching out to others.

Now that my moral compass was turning, I had to figure out how to live. I was a drug pusher married to a woman who loved cocaine and meth, but I was becoming different. How was I supposed to stop doing drugs? Pastor Eddie started counseling me. At first I doubted his sincerity. He was a pastor in charge of hundreds of members. *How could he possibly care about my situation?* But he did. He returned my calls. He texted me scriptures. Through his guidance, I grew to understand that living out my faith was a process I had to take one day at a time.

Then my partner, Lyle, got busted by the feds. We were too close. It would only be a matter of days before they came to my house. I called my children and gave them the number to my lawyer. I knew the feds would try

I GOT THIS

and interrogate them, so I prepared them, too. I didn't have to explain myself too much; they could see all the signs in my lifestyle. Getting all my ducks in line made me swell with gratefulness for Kara. She loved me and begged me to go to church with her instead of judging me. I didn't know where I would have ended up if it wasn't for her.

Then a few nights later, the feds busted my door down while Becky and I were in bed. They handcuffed me in the middle of the night in my pajamas.

"You're going to jail for a long time. You know that, David? You might as well tell us where your stuff is. We might even cut you some slack. Work out a deal."

I sneered at the man. I knew he was trying to play games with me. These guys couldn't cut me a deal. I wasn't stupid. "I want to talk to my lawyer."

I was in a federal holdover before the next day was over. Anxiety ate through my nerves as I snapped into survival mode. I sat and thought about how I was going to get out of this place. My heart beat fast, my pulse thumped in my ears, sweat beaded along my brow.

I was allowed to use the phone one hour a day. I dialed my lawyer and begged him to get me bonded out of there. About the third day, I found out I was surrounded by murderers. One man even made a bomb and blew up a building. I was surrounded by big-time criminals.

Night after night I was woken up by the marshals and questioned. During the day I walked around the cell in a sleepy, anxious haze. The same questions spun over and over in my mind.

EXPOSED

What is my wife doing? Are my children being badgered? Why can't I bond out?

"Get up!" a marshal yelled, jabbing me with his flashlight. He and his partner took me to an interrogation room and sat me in a cold metal chair. I should have been used to the routine by that point, but the lack of sleep tore holes in my resolve.

"We've got something that will make your day," the marshal said.

He clicked on a recorder, and Becky's voice sounded.

"I can't wait to see you again."

"It's only a matter of time," Lyle's voice replied.

My heart jumped into my throat, and tears threatened to break through. They continued chatting. They sounded like frisky high school sweethearts.

"I can't wait to make love to you," she said. The two officers hooted and laughed.

"Are you ready to make a deal?" the marshal asked. I wanted to spit in his face. But instead I slouched silently in my chair.

It was about the eighth day that I realized I was going about it all wrong. *I'm a believer now,* I thought. *I need to put this faith into action.* I got myself a Bible and started reading. I couldn't focus for more than a few minutes at a time. My mind kept snapping back to my wife and Lyle.

About the 10th day, I finally settled in. Reading the Bible broke my hot, feverish anxiety. I read in the Book of Acts about Paul and Silas in jail. They were able to sing songs to God despite their awful situation. What was worse, they didn't even deserve to be there. I, on the other hand, made my own choices that got me in prison. Even though I was a believer, that didn't mean I didn't have to put up with the consequences of my decisions. I stuck to the Bible and prayer, and peace crept over me a little more each day.

After 53 days, I was finally bonded out. The feds sent me straight to rehab for 21 days. It wasn't even a good rehab. The sad fact was that 70 of the 75 people there were heroin addicts. *Is this really happening to me?* I asked myself each day when I woke up. When my time was finally up, I returned home. I was ready to leave Becky, but I needed someone to be by my side as I got through the whole mess. I pretended like she was still my loyal, loving wife, and I didn't make her leave.

I continued to go to church even after my story aired on the news. My first weekend back, I was walking through the lobby when a gentleman stopped me.

"Hey, you're that guy all over the news, aren't you?"

"Yeah, that would be me."

"You're also one of the parking lot guys."

"Yes, that's me."

"Well, we don't care much, we still love ya," he said with a chuckle. "Hospital's for the sick. Church is for the sinners." He patted my back and walked off.

After the service, Pastor Eddie came up to me and shook my hand. "I'm so glad you're back," he said.

"Well, you know, God got me through it. I really couldn't stay away."

EXPOSED

One thing led to another and I was going to testify as a witness in a court case for one of the other guys involved in our drug ring. It was about this time that I found out that there was a hit on me. Someone was paid $75,000 to make sure I was dead. I was put in witness protection for a while and disappeared until the men were caught.

Church members continued to encourage me right until I left to serve my prison sentence. People promised to write me and pray for me. I smiled and thanked them. Up until this point, these people showed me their Christianity with their actions, not just their words. I had no reason to doubt them.

I had been in jail for 53 days. The marshals had nearly broken me down with their tactics, but I made it through. I didn't imagine that my next prison stay could be any worse. I would have to spend 15 months there, which was better than Lyle's sentence. As Becky drove me to the prison, I told myself, *I got this. How bad can it be?*

స్రెస్రెస్రె

The prison guard handed me my bedroll. I changed into my white jumpsuit and tucked the roll under my arm. We walked through a hallway out to the prison entrance. I assumed he would guide me to my cell. Instead the guard opened the gate and pointed across the rec yard. "That's your unit over there. Cell block U, 32. Good luck." He stepped back, and the gate shut behind me. There was a sea of prisoners in khaki jumpsuits between me and the unit. There I was in my stark white uniform with my bedroll, marked as the new guy. *Holy mackerel,* I thought. *What have I gotten myself into?* My brain cracked like a whip back into survival mode. I walked like a tough guy to my cellblock, trying to hide my fear.

"So how does this place operate?" I asked my roommate. I studied people. I hung out with the guys that benefited me. I listened to their advice and did what they said. All the while, I hid my anxiety and fear with a continual scowl. I didn't think I had much choice other than to just follow the flow of things. This was a dangerous place. On top of it all, I felt like a caged animal. Everywhere I looked, there were bars, chain-link fence and razor wire.

One day I sat in the rec yard in the grass and let my thoughts spin. It occurred to me that, again, I was going about things all wrong. *I need to rely on God, not all these Joes,* I thought. I lay back in the grass and looked straight up at the sky. White clouds drifted by. *I'm free,* I thought. *God's up there in heaven, and he has set me free. I don't see razor wire or bars. Just blue sky. I'm free.* The whistle blew, and I got up from the grass and followed the others back to my cellblock. But after that, as best I could, I went about things God's way.

I was thinking I had things figured out, but all the while it was God who had it figured out. I just went all in and threw myself at him. I had nothing but time, and I spent most of it studying the Bible. Church members sent me letters, and Pastor Eddie was one of them.

EXPOSED

I was sitting in the rec yard one day when I noticed this kid hanging around.

He was young, and he wore that anxious, frenzied look. He tried to hide it with that same scowl and a swagger in his walk. But he wasn't fooling me. I got up and went to talk to him.

"You're new, huh?"

"What's it to you?"

"Hey, I'm just making small talk. I was in your spot a few weeks ago."

He looked me up and down.

"I'm David, by the way."

"Jonah," he said with a nod.

We became friends after that day. I repeated everything I read in my leather-bound Bible to him. People started to notice and join us at our table. Some came to heckle and cuss at us. Others just sat and listened. As the weeks passed, even the heckling turned into questions. The questions turned into listening.

"I'm not a lawyer for the Bible," I said. "I don't know who's going to heaven or hell. All I know is that God is as real as you and me. If you take the time to search him out, you will find him."

I told Jonah my story and everything that happened to me. He ended up saying that same prayer to God that I had prayed at the altar. Eddie sent me a Bible, and I gave it to Jonah.

෴෴෴

I GOT THIS

"You know Becky has stopped coming to see me," I told Kara over the phone.

"I figured that much. Word gets around quick in this small town, Dad."

"What's that supposed to mean?" I asked her. "What's going on back home?"

She let out a long sigh. "Dad, she's been going out a whole lot. She still hangs around in that same circle of friends."

I called Kara once a week and got updates. Becky moved out of the house. She continued to run around with my old circle of druggie friends.

It was then that I found out that Lyle was the one who had the hit put out on me. The anxiety came screaming back. My heart beat fast, and I paced the rec yard day after day. At night I covered my head and cried with my fist held to my mouth. "God, please take this awful pain from my heart," I prayed night after night. As usual, I saw signs of his faithfulness.

My 15 months were up, and I gave back my khaki jumpsuit. They say there are two trashcans at the prison exit — one for the cane and one for the Bible. Some men use a disability to get out of work while doing time, but that wasn't me. Some men find religion in prison and quickly ditch it the minute they get out. But that wasn't me, either. I found Christ, not religion, and I found him before I got there. I left with my Bible tucked firmly beneath my arm.

I didn't bother trying to get Becky back. I knew she

was long gone. She was still living that old life, anyway. I did think about her a whole lot, though. I wished a million different horrible things would happen to her. I hoped good and hard that Lyle would get shanked in prison. I wanted nothing more than to see them miserable.

The hateful thoughts nearly ate my days away. I grew weary of it. My mind was like a boxing ring with this vengeance on one side of the ring and all the wonderful hope and faith on the other side. The two could not coexist. "God, take these thoughts from me," I prayed over and over. It wasn't until our church prayed and fasted together that the evil thoughts slipped away. I was relieved and continued the process of moving on with my life.

A member of the church hired me to install custom cabinetry. I was thankful for the job and worked hard. Jerry was understanding when I had to show up late because of random drug tests required while I remained on probation.

Things only got better when Jenny, an old friend from high school, came back into my life. I came across her profile on Facebook and sent her a message. She never did run in the same circles that I did, but we were friends nonetheless.

She was always into her faith growing up. She went to a Catholic church as a child and switched to a non-denominational church as an adult. We started messaging each other back and forth. We moved our conversations to the phone and got to know each other better. We both believed it was a "God thing" crossing paths right as each of us was ready to love someone new. Jenny had been divorced for seven years, and I had been separated from Becky for five years and divorced for one.

I was honest with her and shared my whole story with her. She was honest with me as well about her life. We didn't sit around on the phone telling each other how perfect we were. There were no false pretenses. We discussed what a mess we were. But we also discussed God quite a bit. We shared the same faith, and that's what kept both of our messy lives clean.

Jenny and I married, and between the two of us, we have eight beautiful children and a growing family. When she moved from California to Missouri, one of the first things we did was visit Christian Life Center. The people there welcomed her the same way they did me.

❧❧❧

As I set up chairs for an event, about to head back out to the parking lot, I looked over my list of volunteers. As one of the core volunteers in the parking lot ministry, I have quite a bit of responsibility. Back when I was meeting a different group of guys in a church parking lot to do drugs, I never would have guessed that in the future I would be welcoming people into a church. It's just amazing how God worked things out. Right when I thought I had it all under control, he showed me that he's the one who really had it in his hands. I didn't mind much, because that was the best place for my life to be.

WANTED
THE STORY OF ANNA
WRITTEN BY AUDREY JACKSON

Most of my things fit into the back of the red Ford Escape. I looked over my shoulder at the vehicle parked in the driveway. I stood on the porch stoop, holding a box full of random items I had thrown in haphazardly. I entered the home, its smell and feel familiar, then started up the stairs to the second-story bedroom.

The trip felt more strenuous as I wrapped my arms around the cardboard box holding my belongings.

My feet felt heavy on the steps. Light filtering through the bedroom window welcomed me as I hesitantly walked into my new room.

The sunlight's brightness only reminded me that all of the many objects and decorations weren't mine.

"You can put your stuff over in that closet, Anna." Deb's gentle voice directed me to the closet on one side of the room. I dropped the box of items on the floor.

"Thanks," I said, my voice even and quiet. I caught Deb's glance and forced a small smile.

"Okay, well, I'm going to go down with Don. You can come down for dinner once you get settled in." Her shoes made soft sounds as they hit the tops of the stairs. I plopped down on the bed and looked around. Anger clenched its fist and punched me in the abdomen. This was not my home. This was not my stuff. These were not my parents.

My real parents don't want me, though. So, I guess I better make the best of this.

శేశేశే

People around town knew Deb as the little lady with the two big dogs. You'd often see her walking around the neighborhood streets with her two Great Danes. The first time I met her was in 1992. She had blond hair and glasses, and she stood in front of me as my assigned big sister through the Big Brothers and Big Sisters program in our new town.

Mom and Dad had just divorced, and Mom had moved us back to Missouri to live with her family. Deb was about the age of my mom, but she felt more like a friend and sister. She knew that living in a single-parent home, there wasn't a lot of extra money for outings. She took me to the movies, museums and once she even drove me to a high ropes course outside of our small town. We became our chapter's longest-matched pair. And when the chapter shut down, Deb continued being part of my life, inviting me over to her home and encouraging me to be the best person I could be. Her heart was double her small size. And she gave it away to me entirely.

Moving to Missouri, our life quickly became in sync with that of my grandparents. By moving in with them, we were expected to live the way they did. And so, in third grade, I was sent to church. I was baptized along with my new friends, but I didn't know why I was making that decision. I just liked belonging. It felt nice. The church only consisted of about three or four large families, the pastors being my grandparents' best friends.

We moved around a lot, and I guess you could say we were a nomadic congregation. We migrated from place to place, staying as long as we were welcome. Corner stores. Random warehouses. We worshipped in them all.

Once, when I was still in elementary school, we met for a while in an old, refurbished barn. It was a small area with a stage and pulpit that a carpenter within the church had crafted with his hands. Each Sunday we stacked and un-stacked plastic chairs that grew ice cold in the winter months. The hairs on my arms would stand up straight. And once, I jumped at the sight of a snake coming out of the toilet. I never went in to use the bathroom in that barn again. Despite all that, church as a kid was something stable — something I grew to trust.

കൈകൈ

"I'm going to visit a friend for a week," Mom told my brother and me. But then weeks passed, and we never heard from her. Days went on like normal. I went to school — it was the middle of my senior year — came home and repeated that, until one day I began to understand that something wasn't right.

I sat for hours, leaning my back against the hallway

wall, grasping desperately for any ounce of security I could find. It was solid and still, and much of my life felt like chaotic spinning. I pressed my hand into the floor, feeling the texture of the carpet bristle against my skin. The house was empty, but I kept expecting to hear the footsteps of my mom, returning home from her trip. Silence enveloped the rooms, though, and after weeks of believing she'd come home, I knew she must be gone for good.

We didn't know where she was for the longest time. My grandparents, who had been living in Arizona for years, eventually tracked her down to a prison cell in South Dakota. She was in for credit fraud. And she stayed there for the next two years of my life.

Being a senior in high school, it was pretty obvious that I couldn't live in our home alone, and moving to Arizona so close to graduating wasn't an option in my mind. I couldn't pay the bills in my mom's house, and neither could my brother, though he was 19. So, I moved in with a friend who lived in the next town over, getting rides from friends to and from school, and my brother floated from one friend's house to another. Things were going okay until about three months from graduation, when I got called in to see the principal.

"Anna, I know you've been going through a lot, but it's come to my attention that you are no longer living in the school zone. By law, you are required to attend the school in the zone in which you are living. So, you either have to transfer high schools or find a new place to live."

I looked at him, a burning hatred for my mother rising

up to the top of my head. I felt as if I'd taken a baseball bat to the gut. I wasn't sure if I wanted to scream or cry.

"Sir, I don't have anywhere else to go. I'm about to graduate."

But it seemed there were no exceptions. Not even for kids whose parents desert them. And though Dad hadn't just up and vanished, he had never really been in our lives. And he didn't really want to be.

Later that week, Deb took me out to lunch. Discouragement weighed me down, and my shoulders slumped as I leaned over the table. Sipping on the straw in my drink, I looked across the table at Deb's empathetic face.

"Anna, Don and I have been talking. And we want you to move in with us. There's no sense in you changing schools your senior year. So, if you'd like, we'd love to offer you our home."

A flood of relief came over me. I could feel the rims of my eyes filling with tears, wet and warm.

"Thank you, Deb," I whispered. I felt I could breathe again. Deb and Don allowed me to move in on two conditions. The first, that I graduate high school. The second, that I attend college and make good grades. They encouraged me, pushed me and provided for me in ways I could never have imagined. And later that year, it was the two of them who stood, clapping and cheering as I walked across the graduation stage. My mom was still in prison, and my dad was nowhere to be seen.

EXPOSED

❧❧❧

His dark skin was what first caught my attention. He stood tall at 6 feet, 8 inches. Muscular and dressed in expensive-looking clothing, he leaned up against the bar as I approached my friend Kim and her boyfriend, Thomas. It was an evening in May, and his long-sleeve shirt fit nicely on his strong Army frame.

"Randall, this is my friend Anna," Thomas said.

Randall extended his hand, and my height of 5 feet, 2 inches felt so much shorter and smaller as we shook hands.

"It's nice to meet you, Randall." I averted my eyes and smiled. He was handsome, and the way that he looked at me made me blush.

"Oh, please. Call me Randy."

I smiled up at him. "So, you're in the Army?"

"Yeah, stationed here at the moment. Thomas has been a pal. So, what do you do, Anna?" He gave me his full attention.

"Oh, well, I moved back here a couple years ago. I went to college about four hours from here. When I first moved back, I was working in a residential psychological facility. I'm now working for the state — working with kids in foster care. It's a division of social services. It's been good being back, I guess." My answer felt long and drawn out, but he seemed interested.

"Oh, wow. That's incredible. Well, I'm certainly glad you're here."

It wasn't long before Kim and Thomas were ready to go, leaving Randy and me alone.

"Well, how about you just come to my place and chill out?" he said.

"Okay, well, I guess for a little bit."

Nothing too serious happened that night. We sat on his living room couch and talked. He was easy to talk to. Kind and thoughtful. We exchanged numbers, and a few days later, I texted him.

"Hey, this is Anna."

"Anna. I'm so glad you got in touch. How does dinner sound sometime?"

It started out innocently enough. He was 11 years older than me, but the age didn't seem to put a barrier on conversation or our relationship. Randy knew how to sweet-talk a woman. He'd tell me everything I wanted to hear, and because I had never heard it before from anyone else in my life, I soaked it in like a sponge soaks in water. College had been a time of figuring out who I was — I partied and had a good time. But I had never had a man seriously pursue me, and it made me feel incredibly safe. The sort of safety and affirmation a child feels when they're cradled after a nightmare. For several years, my life had felt much like a nightmare. I kept thinking I would wake up. That one day my life would miraculously have rewound to the years where my family was together. We were like a shattered mirror — somehow all there but cracked in a million different pieces, unable to fully reflect or function.

EXPOSED

Mom had come to my college graduation, but bitterness and anger toward her writhed inside of me. I had demanded that she be there. She hadn't seen me graduate from high school, and though it was obvious she wasn't dependable, she was my mom. And I wanted her to see that I had succeeded. I wanted her to see I had done it without her, and I wanted her to be more than she was. I wanted a lot of things. Dad had really never been in the picture, and my brother Jim had barely spoken to me since I moved in with Deb and Don.

"You're the stuck-up snob of the family now. All you did was get ritzy when you moved in with that ER doctor and his wife. You were handed anything you wanted, while the rest of the family had to work our butts off to get somewhere."

His words felt unjust. Untrue. Deb and Don had certainly helped me, but I had gotten where I was by working hard. Deb and Don had pushed me in the right direction. They had loved me. And that's really all I wanted from the rest of my family.

That's what was most appealing to me about Randy. Sure, he was physically attractive, kind and smart. He was easy to talk to and easy to be with — after all, our best friends were dating each other. On paper, it just seemed to fit. But at the heart of it, he was one of the first people who pursued me. And I was so tired of chasing after the love and affirmation of people who didn't seem to want to stick around. It was like a strong gust of fresh air to find someone who would chase after me.

WANTED

We had only been dating a couple of months when Randy mentioned his bad line of credit.

"Man, I really need to make this purchase, but my line of credit is shot. My divorce ruined me. I'm good for the money. It's so messed up."

"That doesn't seem right."

"Yeah, well, that's how it goes, I guess."

"Can anyone help you?"

"I mean, I'm good for the money. I just need to use someone else's credit card."

"Well, why don't you just use my credit card?" I responded, not thinking much about it.

"Really? You wouldn't mind?"

"No. I mean, you say you have the money, right?"

"Oh, yeah, yeah. I have the money."

"Okay, well, then it's not a huge deal. Just pay me back after the purchase."

One purchase turned into a myriad of different purchases. Randy eventually gave me his checking account number, and each month, I would withdraw money from his account to pay for the charges on my credit card.

I should have known something was suspicious about him. His house had pictures of his ex-wife and four children. I asked him about them once, holding the frame in my hand.

"So, this is your ex-wife and kids? Cute kids. I'm surprised you still have pictures of Tanya considering your divorce was so terrible."

"Oh, those are the only photos I have of the kids." He

would quickly change the subject. I had never known a man to go through a nasty divorce and then keep up pictures of his wife, but I believed his excuses because I wanted them to be true. I believed him simply because he hadn't left. Simply because he was there. On numerous other instances, something inside me questioned who Randy was. He'd take mysterious, quiet phone calls, and when visiting his kids, I'd see charges for items that no one would be purchasing for children. But I pushed that questioning voice in my head down the way you shove a jack-in-the-box down into its hiding place.

That fall, Randy shipped overseas for a short-term assignment. I'd get notices of charges he was making overseas, and more than once I had to contact him and tell him that there wasn't enough money in his checking account for me to pay the bills.

"Go back, and check it now. There's money in there now," he'd say to me. Each time, I'd find money back in his account, having no clue where it came from. Until one day, his checking account number had changed, and I no longer had access to his funds.

"You have to give me back my credit card," I wrote to him. "I can't afford the charges you're making, and I can't access your account." By August of that year, I was more than $16,000 in debt.

᾿ᜆ᾿ᜆ᾿ᜆ

WANTED

I hunched over Randy's computer at my coffee table. Randy had left his laptop with me when he'd flown overseas, and his password was simple to figure out. After a few tries, I was in. In a mere matter of seconds, I had access to all of his files and emails. Something in me told me not to look — to keep assuming he was good for all the things he'd said he was. But I also knew it was time to find out the truth.

I scrolled through his emails until I found what I was looking for — an email from his wife. Randy was a married man with children and a life back in Washington. Apparently, he only needed me for my money. He never wanted me to begin with. My stomach sank the way an anchor sinks and plummets to the bottom of the ocean. I had wanted someone so badly that I chose to ignore the red flags. And I found myself in a sinkhole of debt, discouragement and lies.

❦❦❦

When Randy returned from his tour of duty, he was stationed back in Washington where his wife and children lived. At first, I didn't let him know I had discovered who he really was. I called him and told him I needed him to pay me back, but all I ever got from him was, "I'll send you money. I promise I'll send it soon." Soon never came. He handed me lies and excuses on a silver platter.

Finally, one day, I reached the end of my fuse, and I blew up. "I know about everything, Randy," I told him over the phone. "I know you're still together with your wife, and I know you didn't have bad credit because of the divorce. I also know you never really cared about me. You have a problem. And what you did — all of it was so wrong. I can't even express how wrong it was. I want my money back. You have taken everything from me." My voice grew sharp and loud. "I am sinking. I need you to pay for everything you've charged to my credit card."

He blew me off that day. And for days and days after. He ignored my pleas and demands like he had taken nothing from me.

Really, though, he had taken everything.

When the end of August rolled around, I had blown through most of my savings trying to stay afloat and pay my bills. I was sinking in notices and payment requests. They were all I thought about throughout the day and into the night. And finally, I decided I could no longer do it alone. I knew a lady who was married to an attorney, and I called to see what kind of services he could provide. I wanted to declare bankruptcy.

"Oh, dear. Well, he isn't that kind of attorney, but, Anna, you have got to tell Deb and Don. It's just something you have to do. If you don't tell them, I will."

"No, please don't say anything. They're taking me out for my birthday. I'll tell them then. Just wait a few more days."

I remember dragging myself into the restaurant on my birthday, dreading the thought of telling Deb and Don how stupid I had been. After all, I was intelligent and intuitive — but I allowed it to happen while averting my eyes from the warning signals.

I sat, staring at the menu, wondering if I should order a beer or go ahead and get everything off my chest. I put the menu down and stared at the two people I had grown to call Mom and Dad.

My face must have let the news out before my mouth could, because Deb immediately asked, "What's wrong?" Hearing the compassion in her voice, the floodgates were opened, and I started bawling. My shoulders rolled up and down, the way waves roll upon the shore.

"I don't know what to do," I spit out, after explaining what Randy had done. Deb's voice was resolute.

"You're moving home with us and paying off the debt. That's all there is to it. No more discussion."

She was assertive but not unkind. She knew this would be the only way to get back on my feet. And as hard of a pill as it was to swallow, I knew she was right.

సౌసౌస

Deb and Don gave me $500 to give my landlord notice, and then in October, I moved home. It was a humiliating move — I was in my mid-20s and moving back in with my adopted family because a manipulative man had swindled me. I felt like people were watching me — like they must all wonder how I could have believed Randy. How I could have given him my credit card information. How I could have trusted everything he'd told me. I slipped in and out of depression. My days felt dark and heavy, like the weight of embarrassment and regret would never lift.

I did everything in my power to force Randy to pay the penalty for his actions. I spoke with the military and requested that they garnish his wages, but they couldn't do so without a court order. So, I took him to court, but he didn't show up. The judge granted the full amount. But in the end, they were unable to garnish his wages any more than they already were. It turned out that he had many other children outside of his marriage for whom he was not paying child support.

I kept fighting for what I believed I deserved, until one day I received a letter in the mail. It was from an attorney in Washington, informing me that I was to cease pursuing Randy at once; otherwise he was pressing charges against me. I felt like a boxer after three rounds of punches. I was tired and worn and had no fight left. So, I walked in the front door of my attorney's office, handed him the paper and simply said, "I don't care what you do. I need you to make this go away."

And so, I was stuck with the full debt amount of $16,000.

It was during this time I decided I needed a different sort of comfort. A comfort I had known as a child but perhaps never truly understood. I understood at that moment, though. I was at the bottom of a pit, grasping at sandy ledges. I was popping antidepressant medication each day, hoping that I would somehow be able to pull myself out of the apathetic and lifeless state I was in. Really, though, I needed someone to help lift me up. I needed Jesus.

Sundays became church days. The one day I could sit and feel a peaceful presence. A day where I could remind myself that I was not alone. Christian Life Center became my dose of weekly encouragement. In the beginning, I would sit by myself and be reminded that there was a light at the end of the tunnel. And later, surrounded by a family of believers, I sat and dedicated my life fully to the God who I believed wanted me. Because, really, that's all I was ever seeking. Jesus Christ's love began to fill my heart, and I not only felt loved and pursued, but I felt strong. I could feel God giving me strength each and every day, walking beside me as I worked to pay off the money I had not spent and the debt I did not deserve.

I found that when you ask Jesus to help you, he'll help you in areas you didn't know you wanted him to. He uncovered dark places of my heart and scrubbed away the bitterness. Internally, I could feel Jesus changing my heart toward my mom. I felt lighter and ultimately didn't know how I had been carrying around the weight of anger all of my life.

あるあるあ

My hand felt heavy as I picked up the pen to sign the papers. I sat next to Deb, both of us across the table from the real estate agent. Looking down at the white papers, I could hardly believe what I was signing. Almost four years to the day from when I moved back in with Deb and Don, I was signing my name to purchase my very own home. Deb had been dreaming of this day for a while now — she believed I could purchase my own home. Even after I'd lost everything I owned. She had faith in me I never understood — grace so thick and tangible, you could almost hold it in your hands. After two years of hard work and supportive friends, I'd paid off all $16,000 of debt. And in a few days, I would be walking through the threshold of my very own home. Sitting there next to Deb, I looked over and smiled. My heart danced, and my stomach fluttered with excitement. I believed God had given me the strength to press onward, each and every day. And seeing the light in Deb's eyes, I realized I had always been loved. I had always been wanted.

అఇఅ

I sat at my kitchen table, staring at the card in front of me. It read, "Happy Mother's Day." I'd already signed one for Deb. The other one lay flat, unsigned, and a symbol of all God was doing in my heart. I had purchased a card to send to the woman who had left me alone. The woman who left me with nothing. Who made me feel like I wasn't worth loving. Opening it up, I picked up a pen and signed my name. I could feel God's forgiveness and peace rushing through me. And, in that moment, I knew that he could help me do more than I could possibly imagine.

THE MIRROR
THE STORY OF ELENA
WRITTEN BY AMEERAH COLLINS

I trudged toward my little brother's bed and slumped down alongside him. I picked up the corner of the covers and wiped my eyes with the tattered end. Aaron sat up and eyed me worriedly.

"Elena, what do you think happened?" he scarcely whispered. "Is she coming back?"

I laughed soundlessly, without a trace of humor. "I don't even know, kid. Knowing her, she probably got arrested or something."

Suddenly, hard thumps sounded at the door and snapped us to attention. My eyes flicked to Aaron, and I saw dread completely wash over his face. In that instant, we knew Mom wasn't coming back. We gulped and shut our eyes for a second. We knew those sorts of knocks. The ones that banged with authority, their power resonating throughout the house.

Only cops knocked like that.

෭෭෭

Ever since I was a toddler, I had a mind to take over when things went wrong. I'm not sure where it derived from, but I had a protective instinct.

EXPOSED

Like with my parents. I couldn't stop their constant bickering and never-ending fights. I was too little to step between them as they physically lashed out at one another. But I could hoist my baby brother up on my 3-year-old hip and hide us in a closet — tucking us safely away from the noise and anger. I remember scuffling around the tiny space, stepping on my mother's shoes, as I tried to sit in a comfortable position to hold Aaron. I rocked and hushed him, as my heart pounded with fear.

The fighting didn't end until Dad began leaving the house for months at a time and Mom started having her "guy friends" over. I'm not sure, but I think my parents were separated and in the middle of a divorce. During this time, a man my mother deemed a family friend started finding ways to get me alone. My memories of him are hazy, however, I remember him as Nasty Man.

"I'm so cold." I smothered myself with the thick comforter, but my shoulders hunched as coolness seeped through the material and chilled me. "Mommy! I'm cold. Can you bring me more covers or something?"

Light footsteps pattered toward my room. Light from the hall filtered in as someone eased the door open. I called for Mom, but *he* showed up. Nasty Man didn't have a blanket or sheet in his hand, he just softly shut the door. I inched the comforter to my chin and bunched my fingers in a tight grip over it as he sat at the end of my bed.

"You say you're cold, Elena?" He grabbed the covers and tugged them down. I shivered as the frigid air met my skin. I lowered my eyes while he fumbled with his pants and scooted closer to me. My fists clenched at the sound of his zipper. I knew what he was doing. He was reaching for *it*. He placed himself on me and asked, "Does this make it better?"

"No," I barely whispered.

I simply shut my eyes as he continued to touch me and ask if *it* made me feel better. When he exited the room, I tucked myself back under the covers and cried myself to sleep. I knew what the man did was wrong — private parts were meant to stay private. But, I also believed I shouldn't tell anyone. So, I didn't.

Not all the people who floated through our home were like that man. Mom began bringing over a man named Darryl. He was nicer and friendlier than the others, and he didn't have my father's mean streak. Not long after, Mom moved us to Missouri to live with Darryl.

"He has two daughters," Mom cheerily said from the driver's seat. "Jocelyn is about 5 years old, so just a year younger than you. And Melanie is a year behind Aaron."

"And they're going to be our new sisters?" I titled my head while I eyed Mom.

"Yep." Mom chuckled. "You and Aaron will have sisters."

"And what about Darryl?" My heart thudded as we pulled into a driveway. I thought of my father and all the arguing and fighting he caused. How he left us for months at a time. I wanted real love from a stable father in my life. Someone who wouldn't cast me aside.

"What about him, honey?"

EXPOSED

"Can I … can I call him Dad?"

Mom turned to me and smiled. "Of course, sweetheart. He'd love that."

From kindergarten to third grade, my home life was completely opposite from before going to live with Darryl. After school, my siblings and I returned home to find the house smelling like fabric softener and Mom doing the laundry.

Steadily, the house started getting messy, and my parents didn't pick up after themselves or us anymore. It no longer smelled like fresh laundry, and the skunk-like and earthy odor of marijuana hung in the air. Every morning when we woke up, Mom and Darryl were asleep. I began getting us kids prepared for school, because my parents were too out of it to do it. Even when we got off the bus, they'd be asleep.

We had an awesome neighbor named Rachel Sanderson, who always invited the neighborhood kids over for food and fun with her daughter and husband. She was just a genuine woman who had a natural, sweet, caring and nurturing manner that just drew children toward her.

On Sunday mornings and Wednesday evenings she squished Jocelyn, Melanie, Aaron, myself and other kids in her car and took us to church with her family.

Because of Rachel, I learned about the love and importance of God when I was just a girl in elementary school. Hearing the joyful songs of praise to heaven, being surrounded by people with constant smiles lighting up their faces and listening to speakers talk about Jesus did something to me. It made me feel safe. Church gave me a breather from my home life and how rapidly it was changing due to Mom and Darryl using drugs.

After a while, our parents began locking us out of their bedroom or keeping us outside to play longer than usual so they could feed their habit. Times like these, we went to Rachel's house. We either had dinner with the Sanderson family or just hung out until Mom came for us. I knew Mom and Darryl were trying to hide their drug usage from us kids, but we weren't dumb. Parents always think kids don't know what's going on, but we did.

By this time, my birth father had obtained visitation rights. Whenever Aaron and I visited him, he used drugs in front of us. He was straightforward about his addiction and made no apologies for it. I learned all about one hitters, weed, rolling blunts and the typical behavior of a high person. So, when I saw Mom and Darryl acting all dazed and detached like my father, it confirmed that they were on the same stuff.

One Christmas morning, when I was 12 years old, my siblings and I woke up thrilled, anticipating that we'd get to open our presents and celebrate the holiday.

We ran down the narrow hallway to the living room, then skidded to a halt at what we saw. On the coffee table sat a decorative Santa Claus tray with marijuana piled on top of it. I held my arms out in front of Jocelyn, Melanie and Aaron, silently telling them not to go near it.

Drugs scared us, especially Jocelyn and me. We'd

already gone through the DARE program at school and never wanted to go near the crap. We agreed not to tell anyone outside of our home about our parents, because we didn't want the authorities to separate us. The only one not afraid to face the marijuana was Aaron. Being the only boy, he developed a sort of protectiveness over all us girls, and his toughness came out often.

"Why would they leave this, *this stuff* out in the open like this?" Aaron crossly said. He gently removed my arm from his torso and stepped toward it.

"No!" I whispered to Aaron. "Don't go near it!"

"Yeah." Jocelyn nodded with widened eyes. "Let's just go back to our rooms."

My 10-year-old brother scoffed, "No. The only way it'll hurt us, is if we grow up and start smoking the stuff like *them*. I'm getting rid of it."

Aaron stalked into the room and roughly pushed past the sofa. He snatched up the Santa Claus tray and headed toward the front door. Jocelyn and I exchanged worried glances, then followed his every move. Melanie whimpered a little, and I tucked her against my side.

"C'mon. Let's do this together." Aaron glanced at us over his shoulder and waited for us to join him by the door. Slyly, he said, "Let's dump their pot and watch it blow away in the wind. That'll show them."

The girls and I laughed nervously. When I cracked open the door, we shivered at the blast of cold air. Still, we followed Aaron onto the porch and grinned as he dumped the large pile of marijuana onto the snow-covered ground.

THE MIRROR

It whirled with the snow, and we laughed so hard that we hopped off the porch and started kicking it and tossing it about until we couldn't notice the muddy greenness of the weed mixing with the pure white snow.

Afterward, we returned to our bedrooms as if nothing had ever happened. My parents woke up a few hours later, while my siblings and I were hanging out in my room together. They trudged past our rooms with soft "good mornings" and "Merry Christmas's." My siblings and I looked at one another with sneaky grins as our parents walked down the long hallway.

"Where's our wee — stuff, Paula?" Darryl boomed from the living room.

"Why are you asking me? I didn't do anything with it!" Mom yelled back.

"Well, you must have done something with it. It didn't just get up and walk away."

"Me?" Mom shrieked. "I didn't touch it. You probably forgot what you did with it!"

My siblings and I tumbled on one another and laughed our heads off as our parents continued playing the blame game. "Ha, ha, we threw your pot out!" we jokingly whispered. Our small rebellion was for all the times they'd locked us outside, wouldn't allow us to enter their bedroom or spent nearly all day sleeping off their high. Throwing away their marijuana made us feel victorious over *our* own battle against *their* drug use. While the drugs always seemed to have the upper hand in our family, this time, we finally did.

EXPOSED

❧❧❧

That Christmas morning was one of the sole victories we experienced over marijuana. Over the years, our parents fell deeper into drug use. We later found out they started using meth.

Every time they left the house, we worried whether they would come back to us. If they were gone too long, we prayed the police hadn't arrested them for something involving drugs. When I was about 15 years old, our worst nightmare played out right before us.

Mom left the house to get Melanie a Happy Meal from McDonald's because she was hungry. An hour passed, and Mom still hadn't returned with Melanie's food. Jocelyn and Melanie stayed in their bedroom, while I sat with Aaron on his bed. Scared and unsure why our mom was taking so long, we suddenly heard someone pounding at the front door. We flinched when we heard it, because we knew that sort of knock.

Only cops knocked like that.

Aaron and I scrambled out of the bed and tiptoed to our narrow hallway. As we passed by our stepsisters' bedroom, I shushed them with my finger, then kept walking with my brother. We edged closer to the end of the hallway and looked around the corner. Another piercing knock crashed against the door and jolted it. I flinched, grabbed Aaron and ran to my bedroom where our stepsisters joined us.

We looked out the window and gasped at the number

of police cars surrounding our house. Flashes of red and blue lit up the block, and I quickly closed the blinds. The pounding at the door continued as my siblings and I eased down the narrow hallway again. As soon as we peeked around the corner to the foyer, cops burst in with flashlights and ransacked our home.

"NO! STOP!" I shouted at the police officers as they rummaged through our furniture. I held my siblings behind me with my arms outstretched and just screamed everything I'd ever heard on any TV crime show.

"You can't come in here! You can't do this. Where's your search warrant? What did you do with our mother? WHERE IS SHE?"

"Get back to your room!" A police officer approached us, but we didn't move. He took a threatening step toward us, and we all backed up to our room together. "That's right. Just go to your room, kids."

Jocelyn, Melanie and Aaron sat in a row on my mattress. I slumped against the floor, screaming and crying as we heard the officers search through every room. I'd always felt so protective of my little siblings because I was the oldest. I tended to them more than my parents did, and yet I couldn't protect them from witnessing cops raid our home. I couldn't shield them from seeing our family be ripped apart due to drugs. I couldn't stop anything.

"Stop it, Elena!" One of the cops entered my bedroom, and I recognized him as a man who dated my stepsister's mom for a bit. He scolded me harshly. "You're the oldest one here. I expect you to be strong for them, not lay on the floor and cry."

"NO! You don't understand! They shouldn't have to see this!" I yelled back at him.

"Well, it's happening, Elena." He sighed. "They're not even crying. Why are you crying and keeping up a fuss? You need to be an example for them. Just stop it!"

The police found meth in our house, and my parents got evicted. I didn't know every legal aspect of my parents' situation, I just knew everything had changed. Mom, Darryl and my younger siblings moved in with Darryl's mom in the next town over. Darryl eventually took the fall for the meth charges and went to prison for them, which allowed my mother to get off. I refused to leave, though. I didn't have much, but I didn't want to give up everything over their stupid decisions.

"This is all your fault!" I shouted at Mom and Darryl. "You and your dumb drugs! I'm not leaving. I have high school, I have friends and I have church with Rachel and her family. I don't want to leave just because of what you did!"

My folks didn't initially approve of my desire to stay behind, but I believe they understood my anger. While my stepsisters and brother were okay with going to Darryl's mother's house, Rachel and her family immediately took me in. They cleaned out their college daughter's bedroom and fixed it up just for me. Though the whole town knew about my parents' crimes, and it made me feel so low and unworthy, Rachel made me feel like someone's daughter.

THE MIRROR

The Sandersons didn't see me as the daughter of drug addicts. They didn't view me as the teenage girl who was more of a nanny to her sisters and brother. Their eyes didn't hold pity and judgment toward me. I received nothing but the utmost love, care and support from them. Although they treated me like their own, I still told myself I didn't deserve their care.

Before my parents' run-in with the law, I'd made the cheerleading squad for freshman year. However, I quit because I didn't feel comfortable asking Rachel to do even more for me, like picking me up from practices or games. Rachel was already doing so much for me, why bother her with an unnecessary activity? And who was I kidding? If I hadn't been with Rachel, Mom couldn't be counted on to pick me up, either.

I'll go to school and come home. I'm not good enough for Rachel to spend so much time on me. I'm just a kid wrapped up with my parents' drugs. I don't deserve such love from her.

❧❧❧

After my freshman year ended, my mother informed me it was time I move back in with my family. Soon after, I met Damien. I was 16 years old, and he was 18. He came from a loving, Christian, upper-middle-class family who lived in a nice house. Coming from a dysfunctional family, I just couldn't believe that someone like Damien would date me.

EXPOSED

Months after dating, Damien and I started having sex. I didn't really want to start having sex so young, but I wanted to keep Damien. I figured if he was going to be with me, then I'd just give him what he wanted.

After a while, I believe he picked up on my low self-esteem and vulnerability. Whenever I didn't want to have sex with him, he'd tell me, "I'm disappointed in you, Elena." Straightaway, sadness would overcome me. I wanted so badly to be loved. Growing up, I didn't receive the sort of love I wanted from my birth father, and Mom and Darryl were so strung out on drugs that they couldn't love me properly.

When Damien left for the military, I grew close to his mother, Mrs. Lizzy. Since I'd left Rachel's house, I hadn't gone to church much. But Mrs. Lizzy took me to church with her. She became a sort of spiritual guide to me. She talked to me about opening my heart up to Jesus, living by the Bible and accepting God into my life.

Eventually, I learned to forgive my parents for their issues with drugs and started praying for them. I learned to put my problems in God's hands and to simply trust in him to handle my struggles. Just like with Rachel, I enjoyed my time at church with Mrs. Lizzy, and I wanted nothing to strip me from church again. But when Damien returned, things changed.

I was 17 years old when we got married. The military stationed Damien in Florida, so we moved there. Part of me knew I didn't need to marry Damien, abruptly leave my family at such a young age and move to Florida.

THE MIRROR

However, the other part of me wanted to cater to Damien and his wants and needs. I oftentimes asked him to attend church with me, but he wasn't sure he believed in God.

That confession completely stumped me. How could he not believe in God when he came from such a devout Christian family?

I didn't understand him, but I told myself I needed to respect his wishes as my husband and leave the church world behind. I maintained my relationship with God, prayed to him on a daily basis and tried to show him I still cared. Still, it felt like I'd renounced everything Mrs. Lizzy taught me those months Damien was away.

Two years into our marriage, the dynamics began changing. Damien often lied about little things, I found pictures of other women on his cell phone and had a feeling he was cheating on me. On Christmas Eve, he sat me down.

"Elena, there's something I need to tell you." Damien sat across from me at the dining table, his head lowered. I cocked my head to the side and watched his fingers twist his paper napkin. "It's uh ... it's not so great."

"What is it?" I asked, dreading the answer but needing to know. "Just tell me."

"I ..." He shrugged his shoulders and spat it out. "I slept with someone last night."

"No." I shook my head slowly, but Damien merely nodded. I buried my face in my palms. My eyes stung as I glanced back up at him.

"Elena," he sighed, but said nothing else.

"Why?" I mouthed. *What did I do wrong? Just tell me. Why hurt me like this?*

I threw my hands up as Damien remained silent. But really, what did it matter? Regardless of his explanation, no words could alleviate the feeling in my heart. He cheated on me. He destroyed my trust in him. He ruined *everything*. Even still, his eyes just didn't show enough guilt for his betrayal.

"I can't believe you." My voice cracked, and hot tears slid down my cheeks. "I *followed* you here. Do you get that? I left *everything* for you, and you do this to me? I don't know what's real between us at this point. I don't know where to go from here. I'm just so done right now."

I moved back home with my family for a month and got a divorce. I wasn't over Damien, but I couldn't stay with him. I still loved him, but knowing he shared such intimacy with someone else sickened me. He was my *everything*, and he just tossed it away like my love for him was worth nothing. Everything I knew seemed to be gone. I totally lost my equilibrium.

Right after the divorce became final, Damien contacted me and said he wanted us to try again. Not knowing what else to do, I simply complied. I moved back to Florida, remarried Damien and tried to fix the brokenness between us. When Damien left the Air Force, we moved back to Missouri, and I got pregnant. I was 20 years old.

We worked on our marriage, bought a house together and everything seemed to be okay, until I received a text message from an unidentified number. "Damien had his ex-girlfriend over. He was going to cheat on you, but he felt bad and didn't. Just thought I'd let you know."

An intensity burned within me at that message, but I decided to let it go.

Just months before, my whole world had been turned upside down due to his infidelity. I didn't want to face that again. I was pregnant with our child, I had Damien back and I possessed a deep desire to make my marriage work. I knew I needed to let God completely back into my life. It wasn't enough for me to just pray and study my Bible. I needed to be in the church — surround myself with others who shared a deep love for Christ.

But Damien — I kept telling myself I needed his approval in so much that I did. I wanted him to agree that we needed to invest time in the church, spend time honoring God together and being the sort of Christians his mom taught me and him to be.

Eventually, I talked him into visiting Christian Life Center, the same church his mom attended. When we walked in, the church was having a special ceremony. Many of the members bustled about and slipped sheets of paper on the stage.

"When you're writing the names of your loved ones on these papers," the speaker at the podium said, "think of the ones who truly need Jesus. Think of people who don't have a church home, friends and family to depend on. Write their names down, place it here on the stage and believe God will bring them here."

EXPOSED

As I watched the people walk around the church, I spotted Mrs. Lizzy. My eyes zeroed in on the sheet of paper in her hand, and I could barely make out my name and Damien's on it. I saw the concern on her face as she slipped it on the stage. The way she bowed her head in a sort of silent thanks to God.

I was on her mind. Damien was on her mind. *We* were on her mind. That touched me.

Damien and I left the church that day, not expecting to return. Church wasn't for him. He didn't want to have much to do with it. And I just went along with everything he said about not attending because I knew I had to choose.

I put my husband before God, the one who created me. I'd given my heart to God months before I married Damien, but when Damien came back into my life, I pushed God aside and placed my husband before him. I didn't totally comprehend why, but I felt as if my purpose in life was to please Damien, to be his good wife and act as if our marriage wasn't on the rocks.

How can I keep doing this? Why am I making a god out of him?

When I gave birth to our daughter Kaylee Ann, I found out Damien was still cheating on me. It broke me up inside, but I didn't completely crumble like I did the first time. The more logical side of me knew he was stepping out on me, I just didn't want to believe it. We later talked about our issues and decided we should put the future of our marriage, Damien's struggles to remain faithful and resist temptation, and our financial troubles into the hands of God.

Finally, I believed Damien was beginning to see the light of how important it was to have God as the center of our lives.

We delved right into Christian Life Center and got involved very quickly. I got pregnant again and gave birth to our son Jared, and I felt all was well with us. But once again, out of the blue, Damien surprised me.

"I'm not happy in this marriage," he told me. "I'm not happy with you. I'm not happy with going to church. I was never happy. I only had children because you wanted children. Everything I'm doing is for you, and I just can't take it anymore."

"Where is this coming from?" His sudden confession shocked me. "What are you talking about, Damien? I thought we wanted the same thing. I thought we wanted our marriage to work out and grow in God, together."

He laughed sharply. "You thought wrong, Elena. This has all been a show. I don't believe in God like you do, and I can't put my faith in him like you do. You made me do this. You made me become this bogus Christian guy. Every day for the past year and a half has just been a great big show I've put on for you."

After that dreadful revelation, our marriage fell apart faster and harsher than it ever had before. I stayed with him, just floating through life. I often talked to Mrs. Lizzy and asked her to pray for me. Sometimes my siblings and parents called, asking me if I was okay. I gave the usual,

"Oh, I'm fine. I'm fine. Just been busy with the kids," sort of line.

I just didn't know what to do with my life. I found myself perplexed with God, not angry or upset with him. I just didn't understand why my life was in such a shambles.

"I feel so lost, God. If everything happens for a reason, why is this my life? Why did I marry this man who doesn't love me, who has *never* loved me? Why did I have his children? Why did you make me feel like I was supposed to be with him, and I'm obviously not?"

I questioned God so many times, but I never received the answers I wanted. But something in me, probably God, just told me to keep going to church. It didn't matter that Damien and I had moved to another home and it was 35 miles from Christian Life Center — I believed God pushed me to go. Throughout all the heartache and depression I'd been experiencing over my loveless marriage, I kept going to church. I thought of my children and how I wanted them to grow up with a firm foundation in Christ. I wanted them to know of God from their own mother, not from someone else. I wanted them to have a different life than me, and I believed I needed to keep them in God's house if I ever wanted to achieve that.

One Sunday, the pastor was talking about family and relationships, and it just hit me.

"Your kids are your mirror," the pastor said. "They grow up to live the life you lived in front of them. Everything you do, you are teaching your children to do the same thing. You are their greatest example, their first influence and the one person who they'll always think of when they grow up and experience life."

Oh, my gosh, I thought to myself. *I'm so gloomy. I'm so depressed. I'm so detached. My children, they're seeing all this? No, no, no, this isn't right. I'm teaching my children how to be married, and yet I despise my marriage! If my son ever treated a woman the way his father treats me, I'd never stand for it!*

That Sunday, I knew I needed to change my life. If I couldn't muster the strength to straighten out my life for myself, then I at least needed to do it for my children. I drove to Damien's parents' house that day and confided in them about the loveless marriage between us. I told them I couldn't take his cheating, his disregard for God and his uncommitted approach toward our family anymore.

Surprisingly, they told me they couldn't believe I'd stayed in such a marriage for so long, anyway. It became apparent to me that God didn't want me in a marriage with a man who refused to value me, honor God and put his family before his own selfish desires.

When I arrived home that afternoon, I cornered Damien and said, "I need you to be the man the kids and I deserve. I want you to get back in church. I need you to give your life to God and let him direct our marriage."

"What?" he scoffed. "No. No, I'm not doing that. That's not for me."

"Well, okay, then." I sighed, but stood firm in my decision. "Whenever we argue, we always bring up divorce, so let's just go ahead with it. Our marriage will not get better if we do not put God first and allow him to fix us. If you can't give him that devotion, you need to leave."

Just days later, Damien was gone.

I recommitted my life to God. In my heart, I made a special promise to the Lord that I wouldn't allow another person's decisions or beliefs to affect my relationship with him again.

I refused to put another man before God and allow that man to deter my dedication toward Jesus. It just wasn't worth it. That sort of absence from God only brought about pain, struggle and defeat.

Throughout my childhood, all I wanted was to be properly loved. Instead of seeking total love in Jesus Christ, I thought I could receive it from a man. But Jesus isn't like any man on this earth. He's different. God will never fail me. He'll never desert me. He'll never hurt me.

Some Sundays, as I helped out in the coffee shop at Christian Life Center, I would take a breather to simply laugh, smile and talk to my fellow worshippers about the goodness of God, and I couldn't help but regard my Lord with such awe.

As I welcomed people, I wondered how many times God knocked on the door of my heart and asked me to come in before I finally welcomed him. As I wiped down the countertops, I marveled at how God wiped my many tears away. As I wiped my hands on my apron, I chuckled at how God polished me up and revealed to me my worth.

I never thought I could be a good mother to my

THE MIRROR

children without being married to their father. Who knew I would ever be something more than just "the drug addict's daughter" or "Damien's poor wife"? Who knew someone could actually love me for me?

I believe God knew, just like I believe he always loved me and always will. And that's the love I wanted my kids to see. That's the love I wanted to mirror for my children and for the world.

FAÇADE
THE STORY OF DEREK
WRITTEN BY AUDREY JACKSON

I bent over the bathroom counter. The fingertips of my left hand barely touched the rim of the white ceramic sink, steadying me against the countertop. The blade in my right hand touched the surface of my shoulder. I pressed down and moved it slowly and deliberately against my skin. Blood oozed out slowly, the color of deep red wine. I could feel the pain leaving my body. It didn't hurt — it released the hurt. I couldn't feel the sting or the pressure of the blade. I only felt the fear of being alone floating away, like one of those paper lanterns that float into the sky after you light it.

In the mirror, I could see the blood on my shoulder. And for just a moment, I felt the depression lift, too.

≈≈≈

My story is similar to the stories of so many young people. We sit in classrooms and work afterschool jobs. We walk daily through our list of responsibilities and extracurricular activities. We go to family dinners. Attend church on Sunday mornings. And often, you'd never know we are hurting. We wear masks. Go to parties. Join teams or clubs.

EXPOSED

But something is missing. And we bear the scars of what we feel when we are alone.

❧❧❧

I was born in 1997. The same year Mother Teresa died and Microsoft became the most valuable company in America. I was born into what I guess you'd call a normal Christian family. My parents were supportive and taught me right from wrong. But there are some things that are harder to teach your children. Like how to bear the weight of loneliness and depression. And so, you walk with them as they discover how to deal with it themselves.

I thought I knew God, but I didn't know him fully. So, I guess you could say I didn't know him at all. Not until I knew I needed him.

Mom said I had always been prone to winter depression. But when I turned 12, it hit me hard. I guess some people are just predisposed to it. A lot of people wonder how a kid could feel and experience depression. How someone so young could truly feel so much pain. It creeps up on you, silently. And it steals parts of you that you didn't know you needed. And then you don't know how to get it back. Winter's gray mixes with your spirit, and suddenly you feel lifeless. Apathetic. Lonely. And it makes you pray for the arrival of spring and summer. Your body literally craves the light.

I didn't give Mom and Dad too much trouble as a little kid. But I was always curious. And there's a reason they say curiosity kills the cat. I wanted to figure out my own way. Figure out who I was and what I believed. I wanted to try new things. And so, entering high school, I entered into a new phase of exploration. There were so many new experiences out there — just sitting there waiting for me. Like boxes wrapped and ready for my attention. I began to unwrap them. And before I knew it, I had unwrapped more than I wanted.

꙰꙰꙰

The ground was rocky and muddy. Bobby had taken a bottle of whiskey from his parents' house, and we were out in the middle of nowhere. I wobbled, the whiskey taking over my legs and arms like a puppeteer. I fell, tripping on a stump in the ground, and the voices of my loud and laughing friends surrounded my ears.

"Heyyyy, guys … hand … me … somemoorr."

My words slurred off my lips.

We sat in a circle, my friends passing around a joint they had packed themselves.

"Hey, man. What's it feel like to be high?"

Bobby looked over at me, eyes in a sort of daze. "Yeah, it's great. Go ahead and try it, dude."

I looked down at the joint in his hands, then reached for the offering with my own, muddy from where the ground caught my fall. After my first inhale, I immediately started coughing, lurching my body forward from where I sat perched on a log. It felt as if I was inhaling car fumes.

EXPOSED

Like my entire throat was on fire. My mouth became cotton dry, and I leaned over, pushing my mouth closer to the ground. My insides wanted to come out.

Continuing to cough, I asked, "Bobby, how long will this stuff stay in my system?"

"Two weeks to a month. Not too long. But they say it stays in your hair forever."

I peered down at my old hoodie and dark pants. They reeked of marijuana. I knew I'd have to throw them out. Otherwise, my parents would find out and freak. But my hair? I had never expected it to stay with me that long. My heart began racing. The longer I sat there, the less and less coherent I became. I tapped into a version of myself I didn't know. A fake me. And it terrified me.

かかか

Peer pressure is a real thing. It sounds so stupid — like you should just be able to ignore other people and make your own choices. But the pressure of their comments pressed into me. And I felt the urge to do the things my friends were doing. I didn't smoke a ton, but every now and then I'd join a group of guys going out to let loose a little. Looking back, it wasn't that great. And it wasn't as fun or cool as the guys in movies who sit there and get high. They make you think it'll feel good. But after that split second, it's over. And you're left with a sick body and mind.

Growing up in church, I had always promised myself

that I would remain a virgin until the day I got married. I had really meant it when I'd made that promise to God and to my peers. But then I met Mindy at church camp.

"What's your story?" she boldly said to me one day.

"What do you mean?" I asked.

"I mean, I'm here this week, and I don't know if I fit in. I feel like so many people have it all together. And I don't. I've done a lot of things that other people haven't. Like, I've smoked and drank and done other crap. And I was just wondering what kind of person you were."

"I mean, I've done those things, too. But not a lot of people know that."

I can't tell you what it was about her, but we just clicked. I guess at church camp you feel you need to talk about the things you struggle with. Those things bring you together somehow. But they seemed to bring us together in an unhealthy way. And a few weeks later, in my friend's basement, we crossed a line I'd never intended to go near.

"Let's go off by ourselves," she suggested. Her voice and face were tempting. I think I knew what she wanted. But I didn't have enough strength to tell her no.

I regretted it the moment it was over. Nothing about having sex with her was enjoyable. I felt ashamed and dirty and so far away from the person I wanted to be. The more ashamed I felt, the deeper I sank into depression and drugs and alcohol. It was a cyclical pattern I couldn't figure out how to get out of. I knew what was right, and yet I kept pursuing the things I knew were wrong. And to keep everyone else from finding out, I shut myself away.

EXPOSED

My heart became stone, unable to be touched, changed or affected by anything or anyone.

৵৵৵

I hadn't wanted to talk to my parents about any of it. How could I when they had taught me to live life a certain way and I hadn't listened? How could I tell them I had lost my virginity and partied behind their backs? How could I tell them I hated myself? The drum of my heart beat rapidly. I paced up and down, my secrets screaming for me to let them loose. With a deep sigh, I opened my bedroom door. I was done. I wanted something more.

I saw my parents sitting at the kitchen table at the far end of the house as I walked out of my room. Mom sat on a stool watching television, her head turned away from me. Dad sat next to her, a bulky, tough-looking guy. I walked through the living room that opened to the kitchen, passing our couch and Dad's massage chair.

"Hey, guys, can I talk to you about something?"

As she listened to me share about the past few months of drugs, drinking and the mistake I had made with Mindy, my mother's face dropped, and tears filled her eyes.

"I hate myself for all of it. I hate that I lost my virginity, and I hate that I did things that weren't me. That were against everything you've ever taught me. But please forgive me. Please, Mom and Dad."

They hugged me, and we cried. The way they held my

neck reminded me that there was nothing I could do to make them love me less. More than anything, they wanted me to feel free from the guilt and shame that weighed me down. Telling my parents was a good step toward forgiving myself, but I still didn't know how to be the person I wanted to be.

July rolled around, and it was time for church camp again. It was always held at a place out in the boonies by the river. It was full of winding gravel roads, and the main building where we listened to pastors speak was also the building where we ate our meals.

We called it The Tabernacle, and the old wooden building had this awesome metal siding on all sides of the structure. It was and still is one of my favorite places.

Camp was always a really moving and powerful experience, surrounded by all of my peers, all there for the same purpose — to learn and grow in an understanding of who God is. I didn't feel ashamed while there. I also didn't feel alone.

On the last night of camp, I stood in an auditorium, surrounded by a couple hundred other youth. We sang, our hands raised in the air. I felt the corners of my mouth raise into a smile. Overflowing joy flooded my chest.

After the music, we sat down, and a man came up onstage. He looked out upon the group of us, sitting in our metal folding chairs. Occasionally, he made eye contact with random teens in the room.

"Whether you're young or old, relationships that are unhealthy take a piece of your soul. When you give yourself to another person, you give them a piece of you that you won't get back." My stomach and heart began to flutter. The pastor continued. "And there are many of you here tonight who probably wish you hadn't given a part of you to another person. Maybe it wasn't the right time. Or maybe you gave too much of yourself away. But I'm here to tell you tonight that Jesus Christ can renew you and wash you clean of your regrets and mistakes and baggage."

I buried my head in my knees and began sobbing. Tears fell and soaked my shirt and hands, but I didn't care. I knew my parents were standing in the back of the room, and I stood up and ran to them. They hugged me, knowing that as they watched me cry, I was releasing the burden of regret and guilt I had been bearing.

I could not go back and take my virginity back, but I could be made clean in Christ and save myself for the woman God would one day have for me.

It was an unbelievable and overwhelming joy. My body shook, and I stood there, relishing in the truth that God was willing to accept me for who I was.

࿇࿇࿇

I guess when I stopped drinking and smoking, my friends were afraid to hang out with me. I don't know, maybe they were worried my parents would find out what they were doing and get them busted or something. Either way, when school started in the fall, I felt abandoned and alone. High school can be one of the loneliest places. It's

FAÇADE

like swimming in a sea of faces every day. And it doesn't matter how many people you know — if you don't have anyone swimming beside you, you just kind of get lost.

I tried to reach out to my friends. I'd stop them in the hall or after school or whatever, but they just kind of blew me off. It was like we had never been friends to begin with.

And so, I sank back into a state of depression. My emotions were like an elevator. Constantly going up and down, depending on what button got pushed that day. I locked myself in my room, staring at my computer screen or playing video games. I'd sit completely alone for hours on end. I guess my parents were worried, but I didn't want to deal with it, and they didn't know how to help me. I was starved for friendship and companionship.

The next summer rolled around, and in July, I headed off to camp again. It's funny that I kept going, even when I was so discouraged and depressed.

I think that even though I felt alone — like I didn't have a friend in the world — I also knew that there was more to life than what I was experiencing. And I'm so glad I packed my bags and headed back to camp that summer, because it literally changed my life.

☙☙☙

I had always loved camp. That energy of so many different people in one room who are unashamed of the message of Jesus and his love. But camp that summer was especially uplifting. I met all of these incredible people,

EXPOSED

and though they didn't go to my church, the guys in my dorm that week were awesome. We connected really well, and I hung out with them almost the entire week. I don't know, I guess it was just so refreshing to feel like I was a part of something again. To feel like people actually knew me and liked me and wanted to spend time with me. I don't think people value how big of an impact a sincere conversation or invitation to hang can make.

It was the last night, and I was sitting with the guys from my dorm when the speaker came to the end of his message. I looked out across the crowd, astounded at how many individuals were so intently watching the man up on the stage. *If only everyone would pay this much attention in school.*

As he came to the end of his message, he opened up an invitation for youth and leaders in the auditorium to pray and receive gifts from the Holy Spirit. Growing up in church, I had always heard about God and the Holy Spirit.

I'd read that when we believe in Jesus, we are given spiritual gifts — gifts that are meant to encourage other people, to help them follow Christ. To build them up instead of tear them down and to help us carry the message to those who might not know him.

Speaking in tongues was one of the gifts I'd always read about but never really understood. It was like people were speaking another language, a language that sounded like gibberish and came out of nowhere.

I knew that often people spoke in tongues when God had a special message to give to a group of people. I'd

heard God would suddenly give a man or woman a
"word," as it was often called, and then someone else
would be given the gift of interpretation — to interpret for
the whole group what God was saying through the person
speaking in tongues. I had also heard that sometimes
people are given the gift of speaking in tongues as a sort of
special prayer language between their spirit and God.

All of it just sounded absurd. And hard to even
comprehend. I mean, don't get me wrong, I had prayed
for the gift. I was curious. And if it was something of God,
I definitely wanted it. But after praying a few times to
receive it, I sort of just stopped asking. I didn't understand
it, anyway, so I didn't think I was missing much.

That night, though, something pressed on my chest.

Ask again. Go ahead. Ask again. I felt like God was
nudging me.

The speaker walked down closer to the floor. "If you
ask, you will receive."

The guys from my dorm crowded around me, laying
their hands on my arms and back. The pressure of their
hands gave me a rush of encouragement and eased the
doubt in my mind.

"Lord, God. If this is something you have for me, I
want it. I want to believe that you can and will give me this
gift. I have faith that you will."

The feeling that came over me was like warm honey
flooding my entire body. It just poured out on top of me.
And the words that came out of my mouth were not from
me. But somehow, I understood what was happening, and

EXPOSED

I wasn't afraid. In fact, I was anything but afraid. I was encouraged and completely overwhelmed.

This was proof to me that God was real. And it solidified my belief in God's companionship and love. He had given me a precious gift, so surely he was there for me through everything else I was feeling and experiencing back at home. Surrounded by a dozen praying heads and outstretched hands, I felt anything but alone.

২০২০২০

What's funny to me about my story is that things always seemed to get better before they got worse again. I think that happens sometimes. It's like you think you're on a road with less curves and bumps, then you hit a pothole. I mean, I know I'm still young. And I have a ton of road ahead of me, but I think that's just how life is. It's bumpy and curvy, and you just have to keep driving.

After camp that summer, I spent the next few months in a pretty great state of mind. I felt I had truly been healed and brought out of the dark hole I'd been sinking in for so long. But when I started my senior year of high school that fall, I felt more isolated than ever.

২০২০২০

I saw my group of friends standing in a circle outside of the school. It was time for band camp — the last one of our high school career. I walked up to my friend Jimmy.

FAÇADE

He had been at church camp that summer, and I was encouraged that both of our lives had seemed to change.

"Hey, what's up?" I smiled, surveying the other three guys standing next to him. We had all been really great friends freshman year. But now it felt like they didn't even see me.

"Oh, hey, man."

"Hey."

"Hey, Derek."

They were polite but not friendly. And as the weeks went on, I realized that though they didn't hate me, they had no interest in being my friend. Not in the true sense of the word. They didn't care what I was going through.

The depression slipped back. It clung to me and strapped itself to my back, and I didn't know how to take it off. So I carried it around like a backpack full of heavy rocks. People do that with weights sometimes — carry them and walk with them to make their muscles stronger. This weighed me down, though. It made me turn my head further and further down. And it made me forget that God had always shown up for me in the past. He had revealed himself to me only a few short months before, but I had somehow forgotten. Loneliness clouded my memory, and all I could see was that nobody seemed to want to be my friend.

అఅఅ

EXPOSED

The first time I cut myself with a blade wasn't premeditated. It's not like I woke up that morning and decided to make that particular day the day that I hurt myself. It just sort of happened.

Alone, in my bathroom, I cut my left shoulder and felt nothing. People who haven't experienced the need to cut or the need to harm themselves never understand how you could do something like that. They don't understand how you could literally cause yourself pain.

But it doesn't feel like pain at the time. It feels like freedom. When I saw the blood, it was almost symbolic of something nasty and heavy leaving my body. It distracted me from how much turmoil my insides were feeling. How empty my heart felt. But it's a freedom that doesn't last for long.

I tried cutting on a few other places. My thigh, mostly. And this went on for a couple of months. No one ever knew or suspected. I was really smart in that way — making sure to hop in the shower afterward and clean my cuts. Making sure I never cut myself in a spot where people could see. I would only cut myself on the left side. It made sense to me in my head — it was like there were two different sides to me. The left, covered in cuts and scars, represented what I felt inside. The right side of my body, unharmed, represented what people saw. Smart. Funny. A good Christian guy. I was all of these things at once. And yet no one saw what was underneath the façade I put on. I didn't know how to let that side be known.

FAÇADE

The scars screamed at me as I saw them in the mirror. Each one told a story. A day I'd felt alone. A night I'd wanted to distract myself. They leered at me from the mirror, ugly and loud. I stared at them, leaning my shirtless body over the cold countertop. I can't fully explain it, but it was like I'd been stumbling around a room in the dark and someone suddenly turned on a light bulb. And I saw and remembered that God would not want me to be harming myself. He wants life — full life for his children. And each time I cut myself, I was robbing myself of the fullness I could experience if I'd give my hurts and worries to God. I did believe he was stronger than I was. He could handle what I couldn't. I put the blade down on the counter and, in an instantaneous decision, determined never to cut again.

෭ඁ෭ඁ෭ඁ

I heard someone say once that people are like onions. We have layers and layers to us. And it takes a while to unpeel all of the layers and get to the nitty-gritty of who we are as human beings. We sin. We feel pain. And so often, it's buried underneath all those layers of smiles and hellos. It takes a while to discover who people really are — what they are really struggling with. But I've found that if you open up about your struggles, others will be honest about their own. And in hearing the struggles of other friends — other Christians — it made me feel I wasn't quite so alone. It gave me the strength to tell my parents, who reacted as before, with love and understanding.

"You know there's nothing that can make us stop loving you, don't you?" My dad leaned toward me, elbows on his knees and eyes blinking back tears. "Nothing."

I looked up at him and nodded, too overcome to respond. And the way he looked at me reminded me of something. I never had been alone, despite what I had often felt. And that moment of forgiveness from my dad told me everything I needed to know about God's love for me — it is unconditional, unending and jammed full with forgiveness. After that I knew it was time to start reaching out and sharing what I had learned with others. To start sharing my story with anyone who needed to hear about how God brought me out of hiding and into a new life.

உ‌ஒஒ

Most Sundays, I stayed downstairs working in the kids' ministry at my church. I helped lead them in story time and in songs about Jesus. I enjoyed teaching younger kids. And I can't help but think that it comes from my own struggles. Kids feel pain. Teens can feel dark, empty emotions. And as someone who has been there, I want them to know that there's a God who can walk them through it. I want them to know that you don't have to be an adult to walk with God. I didn't have it all together. I still don't. But I believe in a God who met me right where

FAÇADE

I was. Who saw through the façade I put on for the rest of the world and helped me face who I really was. Who helped me put away the blade and learn to trust him to ease my pain and to see that with God I wasn't alone. Who saw my scars and healed them.

ABOVE THE WAVES
THE STORY OF OLIVIA
WRITTEN BY ALEXINE GARCIA

I was glad for my best friend Kelly's arm entwined in mine. I might have collapsed from grief if she wasn't holding me up.

His face looked stoic, serious. This was not the handsome face I remembered. It was his smile, his constant laughter that made him handsome. His hazel eyes were hidden beneath his eyelids. His tattoos were covered beneath the long sleeves of the suit. I looked sideways at Kelly. Her face was tear-stained, too.

"Go ahead," she said.

"I'm so mad at you," I whispered with gritted teeth.

"I'm going to kick your butt when I see you again," Kelly said. We giggled half-heartedly. It's all we could do to stay sane.

We turned around and walked back to our seats in the front row — the row reserved for the family and closest to the casket.

The music played at his funeral took on new meaning. I didn't have the strength to sing along, but I listened. The fear I felt was like a heavy weight on my chest. I couldn't breathe, much less sing. *You call me out upon the waters ... in oceans deep, my faith will stand.*

I felt like I was being called into a great mysterious

unknown, but I surely wasn't standing. I felt those ocean waves threatening to engulf me.

༜༜༜

It was more than just his hazel eyes and tattoos that caught my attention. He valued family. That was attractive to me. I needed someone in my life who could see my two children as part of his family and not as a burden. He also seemed to share the same moral values as I did. So when he emailed me on the dating site, I gladly responded. It was nice to see a polite message amongst all the "hi, sexy" nonsense.

At first, we just talked on the phone. He talked about his parents and his siblings in every conversation.

We were talking on the phone one evening when it hit me how much he cared about his brother. He talked about him constantly, which didn't bother me.

"We were playing with my brother's fillet knife. You know, the kind that you cut open fish with."

"Yeah, I know what you mean."

"Well, I was sharpening it, or so I told myself, and nearly sliced my finger off. I was bleeding everywhere, but my brother and I were more worried about being in trouble. We weren't supposed to be playing with it, so my brother wrapped my finger with gauze. It was like skin-colored gauze so we thought my mom wouldn't notice. She literally took me by the ear when she saw the blood seeping through."

ABOVE THE WAVES

As usual, my stomach hurt from laughing at his stories.

The first time we met was awkward but not. It felt like we knew each other so well because we had been talking for nearly six months. But I liked him a lot, and he was so handsome. I, on the other hand, felt shy and tongue-tied. I think the only awkward thing about it was me. He decided he wanted to come to my daughter's birthday party, so I met him at a gas station to show him the way to my house. He stepped out of his truck and walked over to my car. He was even more good-looking in person. He towered over me and, with a smile, held his hand out.

"It's so good to finally meet you." Then he pulled me into a hug before I had the chance to say anything. I had to catch my breath and gather my bearings.

"Yes, it's about time, isn't it?" We got back in our cars, and he followed me to my house.

Neither of us was a regular churchgoer when we met. Ryan wasn't the type of guy that had to go around telling people he was a Christian. His lifestyle and the way he treated people said it all. Bible verses were constantly on his lips. When he sat down to read, he would pull out a special book called a concordance, an alphabetical listing of all the important words in the Bible, with explanations and passages where they could be found. He'd use that as a reference and also switch between different translations of the Bible. He said he wanted a full understanding of what he was learning.

We moved in together about a year later. It probably

wasn't a decision that reflected the teachings of our faith, but we were in love. Taking the next step in our relationship just felt right. And a year after that, in 2011, we got married. He loved my son and daughter as though they were his own. They called him Dad, and nobody knew any different.

One day my son Marc got a cold, and Ryan took him to the doctor's office. They were sitting in the waiting room, Marc looking rather miserable, when a lady walked up to them. "Your son is so handsome. He looks just like you."

"Thank you," he said. He looked down and gave Marc a gentle squeeze. He got that compliment all the time. Never once did he refer to the kids as his stepson and stepdaughter. They were his children. Then James was born. Our family was growing, and we were so content.

We attended a nice church but never quite became part of the congregation. We were members just going to church on Sundays.

When we first visited Christian Life Center, however, we were greeted several times. People stopped us to ask who we were. They showed us to the children's ministry, and our kids were welcomed into the Sunday school classes. Hannah and Marc were really learning about God and not just playing games or coloring pictures. The people in this church really seemed to cared about us and, even more so, cared about our kids. After a couple of months, the children's pastor asked us to consider volunteering in the children's classes.

"You guys show up about every Sunday," Stacy said, "and you're so involved here as it is."

"I'll have to think about this and talk to Ryan about it," I answered.

I wasn't sure that we were up for the commitment. But Ryan thought it was a good decision for our family. Before the end of the month, we were helping out. We greeted parents signing in their kids. We welcomed them at the door and made their children feel like part of the group. It was perfect for us. Ryan was so outgoing that many people really loved him.

As our marriage grew stronger, Ryan continued to grow as a father as well. He relied so much on God to get our family through every struggle that came our way. He loved to read the Bible to us and give us little devotionals from time to time. What he really liked to do was pull out his study notes and learn new things in his quiet time. I liked to see him hunched over his notes and books, scribbling away.

కికికి

I went to a church conference one January while Ryan watched the kids. It was a refreshing experience. I came home Saturday evening, dropped Marc and Hannah off at their father's house and went home to relax.

I laid James down on the floor and changed his diaper. He flailed his arms and kicked his legs. He loved to wiggle and laugh while I tried hard to keep him in one place.

EXPOSED

"Will you throw this away, Ryan?" I asked, handing him the rolled-up diaper. He quietly left the room.

Our marriage wasn't perfect, but it was good. We had the occasional squabble about changing the van tires or dirty dishes, but nothing big. So what happened next came as a shock to everyone, mostly to me.

I heard a loud bang and thud in the laundry room. I let out a yelp at first. Ryan was always tinkering with something, and I thought for sure one of his electrical fixes probably went wrong. I left James on the floor and ran over to see what he was messing with.

I never expected to find the scene I walked into. Ryan was lying on the floor, a gun next to him and a bloody hole in the middle of his chest.

"What have you done, Ryan?" I shouted. I fought the rising panic, trying hard to remain calm. He didn't answer. He stared at me with a pained look on his face. His hazel eyes were wide open, looking straight at me.

"Where is the phone?"

He continued to give me that wide-eyed stare. I couldn't find the phone to call for help, and it became apparent that Ryan couldn't talk. Although I was only wearing a tank top and my underwear, having undressed for bed, I didn't take time to grab a robe before running across the street to my neighbor's house. I rang the doorbell repeatedly. "Please help!" I screamed over and over. I banged on the front door with all of my might. No one answered my desperate cries, but I kept trying. "Please, please!" I screamed.

ABOVE THE WAVES

A woman finally answered the door. She looked at me, bewildered, and asked, "Can I help you?" I could see in her face she didn't recognize me.

"I live across the street. My husband shot himself. I need to use your phone," I spat out all in one breath.

"Come in," she said, quickly changing her demeanor. She handed me the phone, and I dialed 911. I gave the dispatcher all of the critical information, then handed my neighbor the phone so she could continue the call.

I ran barefoot and nearly naked back across the street, back to my house and into the laundry room. I was lightheaded and woozy, but it didn't matter. He was still lying there, barely alive. I fell to the ground and placed my hand on the bleeding hole with all of my strength. "Ryan, please don't leave me. Why did you do this? Why?" He had that same pained expression on his face, and no words escaped his lips.

A police officer ran into the room. He threw the handgun down the hall and pushed me out of the way. He looked my husband over and spoke into the radio on his shoulder.

I left the room and picked up James from the floor. I searched for my phone. My emotions were buzzing like neon lights, and a sense of autopilot took over. I needed someone to watch James, so I called Kelly. I needed someone to stay with me, so I called my mom. And I just needed plain help, so I called my pastors. I threw on sweatpants and a jacket as my house filled with uniformed people coming in and out.

EXPOSED

The ambulance and paramedics arrived, and I stood in a lightheaded daze watching as they loaded Ryan onto a gurney. I tried to get in and go to the hospital with him, but the police officer made me stay. "We need you here for more questioning, ma'am."

I walked back into the house and to the living room. A folded paper sitting on top of the lizard cage caught my eye. My heart raced. *A letter from Ryan?* My fingers fumbled while opening the paper. In his neat cursive handwriting was written, "Make sure my son knows I love him. Tell my family I am sorry I couldn't be good enough." I collapsed onto the couch.

"Ma'am, can we ask you a few questions?" a police officer asked while standing over me. My mom walked in the front door. She looked just as bemused as I felt. We met in a tight hug.

The police officer sat down on the couch across from us. "Can you explain to me what happened?"

I recounted the incident starting with the diaper change. I tried to convey the shock of it all, but he was only concerned with facts.

"Did you touch the gun? Did you touch his body?"

I thought they were stupid, senseless questions. I wanted to tell him that his partner could answer all of this. My heart ached to be at the hospital with my husband. He'd been struggling to breathe when they loaded him into the ambulance. There was still a chance that he was alive. Kelly showed up and picked up James. I was glad he didn't have to stay around this chaos anymore.

A detective in a gray suit walked into the house. By this time, the place was swarming with police and paramedics. Flashing lights filled the street.

"Ma'am, my name is Detective Floyd. I would like to ask you a few questions about tonight's events."

Not again, I thought to myself. I answered all the same questions with all the same answers all over again. An hour later, the police finally let me leave for the hospital.

My mom and I got in the car, and I looked over at her. "I have to call his parents."

"Well, you best call them now before it gets any later." The red crime scene tape surrounding the house flapped in the breeze. I went a little dizzy at the idea of talking to his mom.

"Hi, Donna," I said.

"Is everything okay? It's so late." I could tell by her hushed tone that she had been sleeping.

"I don't know how to tell you this, Donna, but Ryan shot himself. He's in the hospital right now." All I heard after that was wailing and crying.

Ryan's father came on the line and said, "I'm going to get her in the car. We'll be there as soon as we can." They lived almost four hours away. Ryan's siblings were coming as well.

When we arrived at the hospital, I was greeted by Jackie, the receptionist. We'd been best friends back in high school but drifted apart. We lived in a small town and so she knew I was there to see Ryan.

"Is he okay?" I asked. I looked her straight in the eyes.

EXPOSED

When you have known a person long enough, it's easy to read his or her expressions. The truth was written all over her face. My pain and fear all materialized in a cold sweat and a ringing in my ears. A sad, dark heaviness settled on my heart.

One question after another flooded my thoughts as my heart clenched up even tighter. Breathing became a task, like I had just sprinted. *How am I going to go on without him? He's not going to be right by my side every day. What will my future look like? What will I say to his family?*

My parents and I were walking through the cold hospital halls to a private waiting room when my pastors Chris and Stacy showed up. They hugged me and greeted my parents. The pain did not subside, but their presence brought a warm sense of relief. I sat down on a couch in the cold, sterile room.

I was used to hospital rooms, but this was different. There was usually a bed on wheels with beeping machines attached to your sick loved one. There was no loved one here, only us mourners. It was surreal. My cognitive self knew exactly what was going on, but the emotional mess inside of me desperately wanted this to be a dream. *How could this be happening to me? I'm only 27. We were supposed to grow old together. I'm never going to be able to love anyone else,* I thought.

My dad fidgeted, his chair squeaking with every move. My mom paced around the room, looking out the window from time to time, shuffling through her purse or applying lotion. They were uneasy and spreading tension through the room. Then, as if the questions running through my own mind weren't enough, she started to ask me stuff like, "Honey, did you see any of this coming? Did he give you any signs? Were you arguing a lot?"

The pastors must have read the anguish on my face. Chris placed his hands on my shoulders and prayed for peace and strength. I hung on every word and whispered, "Yes, God," under my breath. I could, in fact, feel tangible warm peace come over me. The room had quieted to a lull when the nurse came to escort me to my husband's body.

"Was he an organ donor?" she asked. He was. "I want to warn you he won't look like himself," she said. *He won't be himself,* I thought. My mom and dad wanted to come back with me, but it was the calm and composed pastors I needed. Stacy placed her arm in mine, and Chris wrapped his arm around my back. Our tight huddle followed the nurse along a maze of hallways and through double doors.

The sight of him lying on the cold table covered by a sheet made my whole body go weak. I immediately had to sit. Tears came in sporadic bursts. The world suddenly just stopped for me. It just stopped spinning on its axis. It was him lying there, but he certainly didn't look the same, perhaps because his body was an empty shell. I had a certain peace and faith that he was in heaven with Jesus, but that didn't make my own pain any easier.

Fear and anger emerged from the sadness that was already present. Stacy placed her hands on my shoulders and prayed again, "God, I just pray that you look after

Olivia. Take her and hold her close to your heart. She needs all the strength and courage that you can possibly give her, God." I felt her prayers saturate my soul, and I calmed down. I began to accept that this was happening. My husband was really dead.

The nurse came back into the room nearly an hour later. "Ma'am, because your husband is an organ donor, we are going to have to take his body very soon. Would you like a moment alone?"

I would like a thousand more moments alone with him, I thought. I looked through blurry tears at my pastors, then turned to the nurse. "Yes, please." They all left the room, and I sat for a little longer before standing up next to him. I kissed him on the forehead tenderly, despite the anger rising to the surface.

"How could you do this to me? You know I can try and convince our little boy as much as I want about what a good man you are, but this just isn't helping your case much. He just might not believe me because of this." I let the tears flow because there was nothing else I could do. I could kiss him, I could yell and I could cry, but for all the desperation in the world, none of it would bring him back. "You know, when I see you in heaven, I am just going to have to throat punch you," I said with a half-hearted laugh. This was an inside joke between our friends and us. Perhaps I would miss his sense of humor the most.

I walked out of the room and joined my pastors waiting in the hall. We returned to the waiting room and my parents, and there really wasn't much more we could do. It was a silent walk down the hall, to the elevator and through the lobby. It wasn't an awkward silence. We were all lost in our thoughts.

The automatic doors opened, and a cold breeze wisped around me. Phil, a member of our Bible study group, was sitting on a bench outside. Perhaps he didn't know what else to do, but he'd been waiting out there the whole time. He looked me in the eyes and took me into a strong embrace.

"Listen, Olivia, me and my wife just want you to know we're praying for you and your kids. You never have to go through any of this alone. We'll be here for you."

I appreciated him and his kind words. I appreciated my pastors and my parents. And I appreciated the barrage of texts and calls that came over the next few hours. People poured out assurances of support, but at the end of the night, I crawled into bed alone. Desperately alone. I lay awake staring at the ceiling, not crying much, just thinking. Images of his face and his tattooed arms came to mind. I used to trace his tattoos with my index finger when I was bored. He would turn to me and smile.

"What's this one all about?" I once asked, pointing to a black anchor.

"God is my anchor," he said. Bible verses were also written across his arms. "So do not fear, for I am with you; do not be dismayed, for I am your God. I will strengthen you, and help you, I will uphold you with my righteous right hand" (Isaiah 41:10). It was as though he was preaching to me, even from death. But I was afraid.

The night's events played like a video in my mind. I read the note over and over. I tried to think if there was anything I could have done differently.

The next day, the police called me and went back through the same questions again. Did you touch the gun? Did you touch the body? It all felt like a bad dream. I wanted to wake up, but this was my life now. My emotions hollowed out at that thought. Numbness took over.

My older sister flew down from Michigan to be supportive. She drove me to the department store, and we fumbled through racks of clothing. *What does someone wear to her spouse's funeral?* It was so awkward, but I did it. I picked out a drab dress that I never wore again.

The day before the funeral, Stacy showed up to tell the kids what had happened. I was so thankful because I had no idea how to tell them. Hannah was 6, and Marc was 7. I knew how to tell Ryan's parents, our friends and any other adult for that matter. But when I looked at their big eyes, so full of wonder, staring up at me, I had no idea what to say. But Stacy had a magical way with kids. She could get a dozen preschoolers to sit quietly and watch a felt-board lesson.

"Do you guys know what happens after this life?"

"We go to heaven?" Hannah asked.

"Yes, that's exactly right. Do you know what happens in heaven, Marc?"

"We are going to be with Jesus all the time, right?"

"Yes, you're right, too. Your mom and I have to tell you something. You see, your daddy, Ryan, he had an accident. And he is in heaven right now with Jesus." They stared at her in silence for a moment.

"What happened?" Hannah asked. The kids were too small to understand suicide. I didn't even understand it myself. *Why?* still rang in my head over and over. It eventually moved to the background, but I've never stopped wondering. The kids took the news very well.

The surreal mood continued at the funeral. Kelly took me firmly by the arm, and we walked up the aisle together. I looked down into the coffin and wasn't sure what to think. Kelly and I gave each other a sideways glance. Tears stained her face, too. We whispered in angry tones at him. We looked back at each other and half-heartedly laughed. We would miss him, even if we were angry at him.

One person after another shook my hand, apologized, hugged me, cried at the sight of me. This went on throughout the whole day and into the evening. I sat at my mom's house, emotionally exhausted. Feeling hollowed-out was the only thing saving me from perpetual tears.

As the days passed, my fears continued to grow. They were tangible, like an unwelcome guest by my side all the time. I couldn't bear it. I didn't know how to do things on my own. Caring for three children alone. Falling asleep in our bed at night without him. Cooking, picking up the kids from school — all of it seemed so much harder. The house no longer echoed with his constant laughter.

⁊⁊⁊

A week before Ryan died, we'd had a family Bible study. Ryan was teaching the kids about David and Goliath. He took a measuring tape and made marks on the wall in the hallway for the heights of David and Goliath.

"Stand right here, Marc." He took a sharpie and placed a dash for Marc's height. He did the same for himself and Hannah.

"Dad, you're not even close to as tall as Goliath."

"Well, duh. He was a giant." They all stood around giggling as Ryan read the Bible to them and taught them about courage.

But all the courage drained from my face as I watched them playing in front of those marks. I was surprised to see them laughing and giggling.

"Look, Mom," Marc said. "Remember that Dad wasn't as tall as Goliath?"

"Yes, I remember, sweetie."

"He was still really tall, though," Hannah said. Then the three of us laughed together. The two of them reminded me to think about the good things and let go of the sadness. If my kids could do it, then I could, too.

Time continued to pass. When I woke in the mornings, fear quickly greeted me. It felt so heavy, like something palpable sitting on my chest. The weight it caused affected everything I did. I woke up and got the kids ready alone. I took them to school alone. I managed the house and paid the bills alone. I took care of the lawn work alone. I spent my day alone until I picked up the kids. The end of the day when I slipped between the covers was the worst loneliness. No matter how alone I was, I had no desire to be with anyone. As I considered this, though, that undertone of fear crept to the surface of my thoughts. *What if I just won't be able to love someone again?* I thought. *Oh, please, God, help me.*

I dropped James off at the nursery and the kids in Sunday school and sat down in the sanctuary to listen to the sermon. When the band played the song "Oceans" by Hillsong United, my hands rose, and my eyes pinched shut. *I will call upon your name and keep my eyes above the waves,* the people around me sang. Ryan and I used to play this song all the time at the house. Each time I heard the words, a bit of the anguish washed away. I felt it leave. I didn't understand what God was doing, but I could feel him working in my life.

Pastor Eddie stood at the pulpit, and of all the topics, he taught about fear. "There are no perfect people," he said. "If you want to be in a church for perfect people, people who don't drink, don't look at pornography, don't struggle with infidelity, then you are in the wrong place." I looked around. Some people nodded, while others stared down at their laps. "Just like the hospital is for the sick, this church is for sinners. You don't have to be afraid of this life. We are all just going through life like scared people. We hide it well. But God has promised that he overcame this world. He will be by your side if you let him. If you are struggling with fear, you need to come to the front so we can pray for you."

The band played another song, and people trickled

into the aisle one at a time. The front area of the church began to fill. *I'm just like all those other broken people. I am afraid,* I thought. I stood up, and that same warm peace I knew so well, but missed for so long, crept upon me. It spread through me as I walked to the front of the church.

It's going to be okay, I felt God saying to me. I raised my hands and prayed so earnestly.

Oh, God, I'm so afraid. I need your help in the worst way. Please help. The warm peace did not subside. All the time since I had given my life over to Jesus, I never needed him as much as I did in that moment. I felt myself take a hold of him.

As one week after another passed, something happened. My guest, fear, slipped away. But I didn't feel alone. My husband was gone, and I wouldn't see him for a long time. That hurt badly. But I had God in my life, and I believed that everything Pastor Eddie said was true. I could fall on God and completely depend on him. I remembered how he comforted me that day at the hospital, and I drew strength from that.

༄༄༄

I sat reclining in the cushy dentist-like chair. The buzzing of the tattoo gun was loud in my ears. I watched in pain as one word after the other formed in black letters. "She is clothed with strength and dignity and laughs without fear of the future" (Psalm 31:25). It was ironic. I was in immense pain. I feared the future. But there I was, getting a tattoo about laughing at the future. It made sense to me, though. I had no choice but to rise to the occasion. There was no way I could do this on my own. I had no choice but to depend on God and his hand to get me through this messy life.

Whenever I felt the heaviness of fear weighing down on my chest, I looked down at my forearm and read the verse. God had my future in his hands. I didn't like, nor did I understand, the future he had for me. But I began accept that I could get through it. And little by li heavy weight became lighter.

Whenever the kids were sad, the moments they once shared wit his unfinished art project smiling. They faced do the same.

I near
date for tl
supposed
church. We
It was set in
And I
orphanages
oppressively l
needs. It was
others get thro
On the last
alone with God.

located on a busy road in Port-au-Prince. I went up to the balcony with a jar of some of Ryan's ashes. The noise of the crowded streets rose all around me. Hordes of people were walking and bustling by each other, even so late in the evening. Stray dogs barked on almost every corner. Cars honked one after the other.

A surge of emotions rose and fell within me, tears so close to the surface. I didn't know whether to pray or yell at Ryan, so I just did both. "I'm so mad at you. Why did you leave me so soon? You know we were supposed to be on this trip together!" My angry shout was muffled by the noise. I knew he couldn't hear me. I believed he was in heaven, though, and that someday I would talk to him again.

God, the reality is I have to be okay with doing all this [...]ne. I need some hope so badly. You've helped me get [...]ar. Please, I need hope to get through this. Help me [...] be afraid. Afraid of loneliness, taking care of the [...]nces. Help me not to be afraid to love again. My [...]d. I could have gone on and on.

[...]ng sun cast orange rays across the sky. My [...]own, and I opened the jar, threw the ashes [...]e whole horizon seemed to quiet down.

[...]e dogs barking went silent. The people [...]r chatter. We all just shared a quiet [...] caught Ryan's ashes. I had never [...]ch in my life. I guess because of it, [...]s presence at every turn.

ABOVE THE WAVES

❧❧❧

While cooking dinner for the kids one night, I let them play and watch television in the living room. Spaghetti was an easy choice, a dish that goes a long way. I reached across the counter and searched through my drawer to find my wooden spoons. My heart just about stopped as I came across the Mason jar that Ryan was using to make me a receptacle for spare change in the laundry room only days before he left. There it sat, half-done. I chuckled to myself. He was always messing with projects, and the house was still littered with half-finished efforts. Out in the carport was the dragon he was making his mom. In the garage were shelves he was building. I shook my head and laughed as I turned back to the sauce and stirred.

I learned to find joy in small moments, and I reminded myself of the kids. They knew how to let go of the sadness, of his absence, and hold onto the joy of his memory. Those thoughts of him still existed inside of us. And come to think of it, he still existed. I firmly believed his spirit was in heaven, and I would see him again. If you had asked me even months earlier if I could feel this way, I would have laughed at you. But I learned to feel God's hand upon my shoulder, guiding me. I didn't understand what he was doing, and this wasn't the future I would have picked, but I trusted that God had it all in his control. I decided to just keep my head above the waves and let God do the rest.

MEMORIES AND SCARS
THE STORY OF HOLLY
WRITTEN BY AMEERAH COLLINS

Inside and out, you are so scarred. What parent could possibly want a girl like you?

I practically heard the voices clawing at my mind. I carefully shifted my body to exit Mom's car. One foot on the ground, now time for the other. So hard. Everything was such a strain. I hobbled to the porch and leaned against the house as Mom unlocked the door. She eyed me warily, but I just brushed past her. I couldn't look her in the eyes.

It doesn't matter, anyway. You'll never be good enough for her. No one will want you.

I trudged down the narrow hall with my aching limbs. My fingertips brushed against the wall as I tried to balance myself, but it proved useless. My knees buckled, anyway, and I nearly hit the carpet. I'd gone too long this time … too long without eating. I crawled in bed and curled my small form into itself. Cruel whispers scurried across my mind like tiny mice. I clutched my forehead and abruptly choked on a sob when my sleeve slid past my wrist. The bold crimson lines stared back at me. Guiltily, I traced the scabs up and down my arm.

You did this to yourself. The scars. The anorexia. The self-loathing. YOU DID THIS!

"Sweetheart?" My mother knocked, and I quickly yanked my sleeves down. She eased my door open and propped her shoulder against the frame. "Are you okay? You worry me."

"I'm fine." I tucked myself further under the covers and turned my back on her.

"Okay," she barely whispered. "I love you, Holly. I mean it. I really do love you."

Don't believe her lies. Your father, your sister, none of them really loves you. You're not what they want. You're a huge failure. Figure out a way to kill yourself, and the pain will end.

৵৵৵

Growing up in St. Louis, Missouri, my sister Val and I learned about God, his greatness and the importance of keeping a relationship with him. When I was just a small girl toting around Barbies and baby dolls, I knew I wanted to follow my parents' teachings and live my life for God. I just didn't wholly comprehend all the particulars.

When I was 6 years old, I attended kindergarten in a church across from my house. Chase, a boy in my class, knew things other children didn't know. Kissing, touching, hugging and holding, at least the way he wanted to do it, wasn't for children, but he insisted on doing them, anyway. Although my innocent mind didn't have the words to describe him at the time, I later understood he was too sexual for his age. Chase usually gathered me and the other girls, huddled us together and touched us. He pushed us to touch him, too.

When I was a little older, and realized how disgusting the activities were, I told my parents about it, but the damage was already done. I cried and blamed myself for letting it happen to me. I wanted to erase it from my memory, but I couldn't. The memories felt like open wounds, telling me I was nothing but a rotten apple now — a damaged and ruined little thing unable to be whole again.

"Holly." Dad rubbed my back. "That was very nasty and terrible what that boy did." My parents wrapped their arms around me and held me close.

I hiccupped from my previous sobs. "It was my fault. I didn't know. I didn't know."

"Shh," Dad gently shushed me. "I know it's hurting you. I know you think so badly of yourself right now, but Mom and I still love you."

"That's right." Mom swirled a strand of my hair around her finger. "You're our little girl. Just like God and his children, our love for you is unchanging and ever growing. We're just glad you told us. That was very smart of you to do."

Though I could feel the warmth and sincerity of their love, I couldn't understand how they could still love me. I felt tainted. As I peeked up at them, I saw the flash of worry, hurt and even anger blaze in their eyes. Those tender smiles didn't fool me. I recognized the hurt and regret in their creased brows.

EXPOSED

My lips trembled as I lowered my head, and tears dropped onto my clasped hands. I wiped my thumbs over my knuckles, hurriedly brushing the tears away. *How can my parents love me when I hate myself?* I wondered. *How can they love me as much as Val when these things didn't happen to her? They don't get what I'm feeling. They don't know how much this hurts.*

As I grew older, I continued to view myself as a failure. A stinging sadness flooded my entire being, and every day became a struggle. I thought the kindergarten incidents were my personal screw-ups. I believed it was solely my fault for letting Chase talk me into messing around with him. I should have spoken up. I should have screamed. I should have pushed him away and run to a teacher. But I didn't. And I couldn't understand why — I just didn't.

When my parents tried to show me love and say Chase was the sick one who needed help, not me, I rejected their efforts to reassure me. My parents simply wanted to make me feel better, I thought. They didn't want to really deal with my tears, pouts and bursts of anger. I thought their words were just meant to soothe me, their damaged daughter.

As a preteen, I developed an eating disorder and struggled with low self-esteem. For days, I refused to eat anything. Part of me wanted to starve to death, while the other half just lacked the motivation or basic desire to eat. Sometimes I went so long without food that I could barely open doors or get in and out of cars. I crawled to my room and cried into my pillow when my bones ached. When walking through the house proved to be too difficult, I just lay across my bed. My anorexia wasn't the only damage I did, though.

I cut.

I hated it, but I loved it. I needed to feel the cold blade against my skin, but I wanted to chuck it in the trash, too. The red blood oozing out and trickling down my arms offered solace, but I stretched my sleeves over my palms and ensured no one ever found out. In that moment, when the sharpness swiped against my skin, I gained control over my troubles. *I* made the decision to harm myself. *Me*. Not anyone else. Still, I felt ashamed of my dirty secret.

Knowing what I did in the dark, away from my family's eyes, depressed me even more. I hated my reflection. The hardened face that stared back at me did nothing to ease my pain. My tired eyes, pale skin and scars running up and down my body just looked so *ugh*. I didn't deem myself beautiful or worthy of anything but pain and destruction. So I put my energy into destroying my body. The outward me needed to be as crushed and shattered as the inward me.

I told myself I'd never be good enough for my mother, father or Val. It didn't matter how many times they expressed their love for me. It didn't matter how much Val tried to include me in her life. None of their caring acts healed me. Sinister voices seemed to whisper in my ears how worthless I was.

I knew about God. My parents and church taught me to always depend on him for help and guidance. I'd heard

EXPOSED

God was able to take away pain, but as a young girl, all I could do was focus on the ache I felt. I still believed in God. I still loved God. Nothing could ever replace him. But I just didn't trust him with my problems. I didn't give them to him to fix. Instead, every night I climbed in bed and contemplated the best ways to commit suicide.

"How can I end my life?" I picked at my pillow with my thin fingers. "What can I do? Should I use a blade? Should I use medicine? What is the best way to go?"

I had no idea, but I vowed to find out.

ॐॐॐ

My parents moved our family to the country and started a church in our home. I was still dealing with my insecurities, but I'd found out self-harm wasn't the way to address my issues. Also, since my parents kept church in my life, I wanted to please God. I figured hurting myself wasn't something God would like.

The church outgrew our home, the congregation hired a pastor and I turned 13.

Still, negative feelings crowded my head. I'd made plenty of friends, but I had a hard time connecting with them. I didn't want to develop such close bonds with them that they ended up seeing how much I hated myself. Unable to have the physical, face-to-face connection with my peers, I threw myself into online chat rooms and social media sites.

Every day I sat behind the computer and lived my life through the Web. That's how I met Jonathan when I turned 16. He was a few years older than me and lived in North Carolina, but we just seemed to click as friends. Jonathan participated in his church's functions so often that he hoped to become a pastor one day. After a while, he became a close confidant who never failed to offer an uplifting word to encourage me or remind me how much God loved me.

"You just need to completely give your past to God, Holly," Jonathan messaged me one afternoon after I'd told him about some emotional troubles I'd been experiencing.

I stared at the keyboard and sighed.

"I'm trying," I typed. "It's hard. These feelings, they just seem so inescapable. Like they'll always be here. The pain will never leave."

"You have to believe otherwise. Even when it seems the complete opposite, you have to believe you'll be whole again."

"I know. Can you just pray with me?" I asked.

"For sure. Always," he sent with a smiley face.

Jonathan eventually moved to Missouri for college. There were still quite a few miles between us, so every weekend my family picked him up and brought him to church with us. We began dating, and it seemed like our relationship was perfect. One rainy Sunday, that all changed. Jonathan was driving my parents' car back from our errand at Walmart, but he refused to turn the windshield wipers on. His driving unnerved me. I'd experienced car accidents before, and I became annoyed and frantic when folks drove recklessly.

"Hey." I squinted out the window, trying to see through the blurriness the rain created. "Why don't you turn the windshield wipers on, Jonathan? It's pouring down."

He cut his eyes at me. "It's fine, Holly. I can see."

"Well, it's really scaring me. Can you just turn them on for my sake?"

"Why?" His voice heightened. "I can see just fine. Just because you can't see, doesn't mean I can't. You're not the one with the license here, I am. I don't need them on just yet."

"All right, geez." I sighed. "I'm sorry. I didn't mean to make you angry."

"Well, you did. You're always nagging me about petty stuff. Just leave it be!"

Nagging? What is he even talking about? I wondered. *He's just mad for no reason. I need to settle him down. I don't want him to be upset with me. Not him. I can't lose him.*

"Okay." I lightly touched his shoulder, but he shrugged it off. "Just calm down, Jonathan. You're going home today. I don't want our weekend to end on a bad note."

"It's a little too late for that." He tightened his grip on the steering wheel as the rain pattered against the window even more.

"No, it's not!" I smiled, desperately trying to lighten the atmosphere. "Is there anything I can do to make you feel better? How about we pull over and dance in the rain?

My dad used to do that all the time with Mom, Val and me. It'll be fun!"

Jonathan huffed, but pulled down a country road a few minutes from my home. When I grabbed the handle to get out of the car, he immediately placed his hand at the back of my neck and gripped me. I winced at the pressure and jerked my head to the side. Still, he didn't lighten his hold.

"What are you doing?" I pushed at his wrist. "That hurts."

"We're not going anywhere." He leaned over the center console. "You're going to do something for me to make me feel better. That is what you want, right? For me to feel better?"

His free hand went to his slacks. He eyed me with a raised brow, but I couldn't answer. I just sat there, not understanding why he unfastened his pants. He knew about my vow of purity, a promise to God to abstain from sex until marriage, and he knew I'd never break it.

I froze. Unable to move. Unable to speak. Unable to shout "NO!"

"Dancing in the rain won't make me happy," he said gravely. "Only this will."

Jonathan shoved my head down. He forced me to perform a sexual act on him. I wanted to scream, but my voice had suddenly shut down. My whole body convulsed in my seat, but I couldn't wrench myself away from his impossible hold. I was terrified. When it was over, I flung myself out of the car, rammed my finger down my throat and tried to throw up.

EXPOSED

"WHAT IS WRONG WITH YOU?" I finally screamed as I dry heaved and cried. I glared at him in the driver's seat. His pants were fastened. He looked at me with widened eyes and parted lips. "ANSWER ME! WHY DID YOU DO THAT?" Unable to vomit, I whirled on him. "How could you do that to me? I can't believe you, Jonathan."

"You didn't exactly pull away, Holly," he mumbled.

"I couldn't!" I shouted. "I was scared, I was shocked, you were pushing me down, I was — you know what? Screw it!" I hopped into the car and slammed my fist onto the dashboard. "You're sick! That was disgusting. I hated it! You hear me? I HATED IT!" When he didn't start the car, I screamed in his face. "Drive! I'm ready to go home. Just take me home."

Jonathan unsteadily started the car, but he was so shaken up about what he'd done that he accidentally drove us into a ditch. I called Val and Dad to help us, and when they arrived, I knew they could tell something was off about me, but I didn't tell them what happened.

"Hey." Val pulled me aside, and her eyes swept over my face. "What's wrong, Holly? You don't look so good." When I simply shook my head, she asked, "Did he try anything? Did he hurt you?"

"No, Val," I tried to reassure her. "I'm fine."

I wanted nothing to do with Jonathan after that. We still went to the same church, but I just felt so uncomfortable around him and any man for that matter. I was so embarrassed and angry that I didn't tell anyone what happened, until three months later when I broke down to my mother and told her everything.

"I didn't want to do it, Mom. I just froze." I slumped over my lap as I sat on her bed. She pulled me to her side and hugged me as tears slid down my cheeks into my lap. "It was like everything in me wanted to scream, push him away or just yell for him to get his hands off me. But I just couldn't move. I couldn't talk. I couldn't do anything."

"Hey. You look at me, Holly." Mom tugged my face close to hers and used her thumbs to wipe my tears away, trying to hold back her own. "This was not your fault, honey. I know it was hard coming to me about this, but just know that I don't look at you differently or feel a certain way about you."

"But I should have done something!" I clenched my fists and dug my nails into my palms.

"Sometimes people just freeze up, Holly." Mom hugged my trembling body.

"Please don't tell Val and Dad. I'm not ready for them to know. I'm so ashamed. I should have fought harder. I should have forced myself to back away. I should have done so much."

"Listen to me." Mom pulled my forehead against hers. "What happened does not define who you are. It just happened. When we do tell your father and sister, I know they will feel the same way. For now, we'll keep this between us. Jonathan is no longer in your life, okay?"

I nodded.

"The only cruel and disgusting person in this matter is

Jonathan. It's not you, Holly. Even when you were a little girl, it was never you."

"I know," I whimpered, but it came out so cracked and broken. "I know that now."

"And I know it feels so far-fetched and impossible right now, honey, but one day God will use this horrible incident for something good in your future. We don't know why these things happen. Just know that God is always there. He'll never let you experience anything he knows you truly cannot handle. Don't lose your belief in God. Don't think he has forgotten you or left you in pain. He's here. He's always here."

I hung my head in shame for a year, just so disgusted with myself. *How could I come from such a loving and caring home and let such cruelty happen to me?* I didn't understand. I tried to be a good girl, and yet I felt like I always got dealt an ugly card. I just didn't get it.

I tried my hardest to believe in God's love for me, but sometimes the ache of what happened just cut me so deeply. I wanted to believe he was there, but every so often, I wondered if he heard my cries. I reminded myself that God wouldn't let any hardship in my life ruin me, but I already felt so damaged. The memories of it pained me.

But I refused to give up on God.

༄༄༄

After Jonathan betrayed my trust, I plunged myself into church. By senior year of high school, I was a singer on the praise and worship team. Every Sunday I expressed my love and gratitude toward God through songs. I'd joined the church student council and served as a teacher for the younger children.

Singing to God helped me overcome so many of the memories of my past. I didn't allow what happened with Chase or Jonathan power over my emotions or dictate how I viewed myself anymore. Even as a young adult, I harbored shame, a dislike toward myself, and didn't trust many people outside of my family. But I believed God was slowly mending the brokenness inside me. It was like every time I sang, I was dedicating my vocals to heaven and asking God to envelop me in his arms and assure me everything would be okay.

Everything I did at church, I did it for Jesus. I was no longer that little girl who just wanted to live for God and adhere to my parents' teachings. I truly desired to please God and make him happy. Besides living according to the Bible, becoming so involved in church activities was how I served God, too. I was growing in God, and I loved the feeling of it.

With such a new outlook on my relationship and dedication toward God, I decided to volunteer at a youth camp for children who had suffered abuse. Helping there presented me with a whole new perspective on my past. So many children, as young as 6 years old, had been mentally, physical or sexually abused. What made their situations so much heavier than my own was that many of their parents or trusted family members were the abusers. I couldn't imagine growing up without the love expressed by my family.

A liberated feeling came over me during my week at that camp. I felt like I needed to share my story back home and allow it to help other kids who'd been misused just like I had. Some young people didn't know God could heal their wounds and put their broken pieces back together. I wanted to share that knowledge with them. I didn't know exactly what good could come out of telling my story, but I figured God knew. Before I returned home, I told our mission team about my abuse.

"When I was a little girl, something happened to me." I tucked my shaking hands in my lap and peered at a couple of our church's deacons on the couch across from me. "And recently, well, a few months ago actually, I experienced sexual abuse, and it impacted me pretty badly. I want to say I'm over it, but I'm not."

"Holly." One of the deacon's wives smiled with sincerity. "I can tell your story was very hurtful, and I'm so sorry that happened to you. I think you should let God use your story to reach others who have been harmed."

"I agree," her husband urged. "I believe you should tell our church family. Let God use your past to bring others to his son, Jesus. Let people know they're not alone in their hurt, and there is someone who can take the pain away."

I returned home from camp with such a revived spirit. But when I shared my story with my church family one Sunday, the pastor became so angry with me.

He took me to the back office and practically yelled at me. "Why would you share that story with people?" He slammed his hands on the mahogany desk, and I flinched at the harshness in his tone. "What is wrong with you, Holly? You're an embarrassment! I can't have someone like you singing in front of the church every Sunday morning. How dare you divulge that with the people here! No one wants to hear that! You're obviously too fragile."

"It, it was a testimony. My story of what God did for me." My voice shook. "I didn't realize you would be angry. I wanted to reach people who may have been through similar things. I never meant to cause trouble."

"You've caused a stir with this congregation." He sat in his chair and rubbed at his forehead. "I have no choice but to relieve you from your duties. You are no longer a singer on the praise and worship team."

"What?" My heart dropped. "No, no, you can't do that!"

"You can forget about your teaching position for the children's church. And you're kicked off the student council. I'm sorry, Holly, but I can't have you speak about sexual abuse so freely and expect to continue serving in God's house. It makes me look bad."

When I left church that day, all the strength, courage and happiness I'd built up over the past couple of months was just stripped away within a matter of minutes. Depression came back with such a tight grip, too.

My entire family was eventually voted out of the church. The one *my* parents started in *our* home just a few years prior. There were some members who didn't agree with what happened to my family, but I still felt so ostracized by everyone. Some of my closest friends voted to kick us out of the church we had started. I believed all they saw when they looked at me was a dumb little girl who'd been sexually abused and had the audacity to tell about it. All they saw was my past.

As usual, my parents and Val didn't blame me for what happened. They expressed their love and support of me and my decision to share my story. However, their love for me couldn't change the effects this boot from the church had on me. Their love couldn't erase the cloud of darkness that, once again, took up residence over my life. I truly thought I was of no value.

The rejection by the leaders of the church shattered me. They stole the most favorite and constant element of my entire life. They hurt me so badly, and I vowed to never step foot in any church again.

༒༒༒

Months later, I graduated from high school and started college. A year slowly passed, and I had yet to return to church. Everything was so surreal. I'd been so accustomed to attending church on Sunday mornings and even throughout the week. The absence of church in my life created a sort of void. I still possessed a deep reverence for God, but I wanted nothing to do with meeting with other people of faith. Getting tossed aside had snatched away so much more. I couldn't sing to God the way I wanted to. I felt so unworthy to sing to him that I stopped.

My connection with God was still alive, but it was different. There is something about celebrating life in Jesus Christ with other people who love God and just being in God's house that strikes something within a person. I desired the feelings I once experienced in church, but there was no way I'd ever go back. I vowed I'd never let them hurt me again.

Sometimes I misdirected my anger toward God for allowing that situation to happen. I believed God placed it on my heart to share my story, and yet I was rejected for it. If God knew that would happen, why put me in that predicament? My parents always taught me to trust in God, to depend on him and understand he always has a plan. They always said that even when the devil tries to destroy me, there is only so much he can do to a child of God before the Lord steps in and tells him, "That's enough." So when darkness consumed me in every corner of my life, I chose to believe God had already devised a plan to ease my troubles.

But how can any of this be used for something good? I often asked myself. *What sort of plan does God have for me that I have to endure such hurt? I don't understand why he let the church be so cruel to my family.*

When I couldn't grasp why God let me undergo such pain, I often told him, "God, you're giving me way too much. You have more confidence in me than I have in myself. I don't understand you." I soon realized it wasn't my place to question God or try to completely understand his thinking. I was his daughter. I just needed to let him be my heavenly father.

Eventually, my parents started another home church. I was almost 20 years old, and the idea of my parents doing that again terrified me. When the services started, I went because I knew supporting my parents was the right thing to do. So many people from our previous church attended the services, and they expressed how they disagreed with what the pastor and members did to my family and me. I couldn't believe how much support and love they poured out on me. They even encouraged me to start singing again. A few Sundays here and there, I sang praises to God and found my voice again. Over time, I saw how God erased the fear and feelings of unworthiness about myself.

༨༨༨

In my early 20s, I moved back to St. Louis to finish my college education. I'd taken a break for a year or so and decided it was time I finished what I'd started. While in college, I couldn't find quite the right church for me. I was so used to expressing my love for God so freely within my parents' church. Finding a church where I felt that home-like connection proved hard.

I ended up stumbling upon a particular church where the essence of pure hope, love and familial connection seemed to just rest in the air. Another aspect that made the church so different was that I was able to experience

MEMORIES AND SCARS

God from the pews instead of the platform. Usually I was the one singing and getting the membership fired up for God, but I was able to listen to other people sing and participate in the service. The church really expanded my knowledge of God and helped me get closer to him.

During that time, I usually traveled back to Rolla to visit my family, but I always had to pass where Jonathan pulled off in the rain with me. Ever since the incident, I tried to avoid driving down that road or even looking at it. I just sped past it to my parents' house. One evening, I was driving back and nearing that certain road, and I heard a voice clearly instruct me, *Turn down the road.*

I immediately trusted it was God's voice. I could hear him so clearly, like he was speaking right into my ear. I just couldn't believe he actually wanted me to turn down *that* road. He knew what happened there. He knew the years of hurt and shame that developed from that one incident. Why would he have me drive on that road?

"Um, God," I said in the car. "I love you. I trust you. But, this is not happening. No way."

Yes. Turn.

"Okay, God." I sharply laughed and scanned my surroundings. I'd be approaching that side road any minute, and I did not want to turn down it. "Don't take this the wrong way, but you've got to be out of your mind. I cannot go down that road. Please don't make me."

Again, I felt God push me to follow him. *Go, Holly. You have to trust me. You have to turn.* At the last second, I jerked onto that side road and pulled over. I cried out to

Jesus and asked him to fully take away the pain Jonathan had forced upon me. I asked him for true peace and felt God give it to me. I felt a rush of such serenity wash over me. I still felt the hurt of what happened, but I had a sense of freedom. That road no longer controlled me. God showed me that I could revisit my past, even the places those horrible things happened, and he'd give me strength and courage to face it and move past it. All I had to do was trust him.

I may have hesitated and resisted when God first prodded me to obey, but moments later, I completely put my faith in God's instructions. I trusted Jesus to be with me as I drove down that road, and I could practically feel him wiping my tears away and telling me I didn't need to cry over the past anymore. I realized that if God could heal me from that horrific part of my life, what more could I trust him with?

I started singing to God in my car. I asked him to let his love, gracious spirit and favor just rain down on me. *Open the floodgates of heaven, Lord. Let it rain.* I sang to Jesus on that road.

After I made it to my parents' house, I stepped inside. Quiet. I immediately dropped to the kitchen floor on my knees and started screaming, "No! No! No!" I shouted it so loudly and with such conviction. I knew those were the words, and the power in which I needed to yell them, I had wanted to scream at Jonathan years before. I couldn't speak in that moment with him. I couldn't even move. I was so scared that I became paralyzed during his forceful demands. My screams in the kitchen were such a great release. I knew Jonathan didn't hear me, but I believed God did.

The next year, I moved back to Rolla near my family. God had elevated my self-esteem and helped me to open myself back up to people again. I reconnected with an old friend. Ben and I knew each other from my younger years when I was really focused on becoming a singer. He had a band, and I had a voice. We always said we'd work together one day. However, we each had some personal issues we needed to overcome, and we put our music dreams on hold. We kept in touch off and on, but after a while, we drifted apart.

One day, Ben called me out of the blue. Problems in life had taken a toll on him. Just hearing his low, dragging voice, I could hear the heartbreak and pain in his words. I stayed on the phone with him and told him about Jesus and how he could solve his problems. I opened up about my past and how God brought me out of every obstacle.

One week later, Ben called me. He said he'd given his life to God. I invited him to church, and we started going to services together. Soon after, we started dating. In my heart, I knew Ben was different from Jonathan. Maybe it's because he openly bared his heart to me during his lowest moments and allowed Jesus to come in and heal him. Or perhaps it's because he listened closely to me, taught me self-defense and showed disgust toward men who abused women. I just knew he was different.

During our self-defense sessions, he challenged me

and coached me through every step. But he also stressed his utmost care for me and showed me he wasn't the bad guy.

Ben placed my back against the gym wall and flattened his palm beside my head. He leaned into me with his head tucked near my ear. "If you're in a position like this, you need to shoot for a soft body target. It doesn't matter how strong a man is or how often he works out, there will always be parts of his body that are weaknesses. Like the throat and eyes."

"Right." I nodded firmly. "Got it."

"Good. Now what you're going to do for this position is thrust your arm out, push your fingers into his esophagus, then dig down. Just jab forward, slant down and hook onto him. This will choke him. All right?" Ben watched me nod again. Something flashed within his eyes, and he abruptly stepped back. He tucked a strand of hair behind my ear and palmed my face. "I know this may seem uncomfortable right now, me being this close to you, but remember it's just me. I won't hurt you."

I laughed softly. "I know you won't, Ben."

"This is how it'll be if your attacker is looming over you. The jerk will leave no room for you to escape — his goal is to trap you. I just want you to know these things. You know?"

Before I could answer, Ben shot toward me. I instantly struck my arm out, pushed into his throat and dug down. He immediately coughed, backed away and slumped over. He rubbed at his neck and stared at me.

MEMORIES AND SCARS

"Oh, my gosh! Did I hurt you?" I shrieked. "You surprised me!"

He grinned. "As will an attacker, Holly. You did good, almost perfect." Ben straightened and grabbed my shoulders. He gently pushed me to the wall again. "But don't lose your position on the wall with this technique. If your arm is straight out, and he tries to push you back, you have nowhere to go. Your fingers simply jab deeper into his esophagus. Moving forward will just get him choked even more. So, instinctively, he'll back off before thinking to try anything else on you. And that's when you knee him in the groin and run off."

"Wow." I ran my fingers through my hair. "Why couldn't I have known this before? With *him.*"

"Hey." He wound our fingers together and looked me in my eyes. "You know it now. I'm teaching you. Nothing like that will happen again. I promise I'll protect you and teach you to protect yourself."

Whenever Ben looked at me like that, I knew he meant it. He wouldn't use my vulnerability against me. He wouldn't boot me out of his life because of my abusive past. He didn't expect sexual relations out of me. He respected and shared my love for Christ. Everything with Ben just felt so natural and easy.

He became my best friend and then my fiancé. He loved me for me, with all my scars and painful memories. Sometimes if we argued, I automatically expected him to leave me because I'd never had someone outside of my family truly love me the way he did. Someone who overlooked my faults and didn't take the first chance to leave me when I did something wrong.

"Do you even know what love is, Holly?" Ben asked me once.

"I think so," I replied, unsure.

Every day, Ben showed me the true definition of love. He dropped everything and stayed with me when I was sick. When nightmares and sleep paralysis took hold of me in the dead of the night, Ben arrived the next day and prayed throughout my home.

Ben was simply *there*, and he wanted to be. I never imagined that sort of unconditional love was possible except from Jesus and my family.

We became engaged on the same date Jonathan took advantage of me. Not only did God give me a future husband who wanted only to protect me, but he replaced that horrific date with an incredible memory. It would no longer stand as the most despised day of my past, but as a loving date that jumpstarted my future with Ben.

It amazed me how God gave me someone like Ben. And I came to be so grateful for my family sticking by my side during my worst times. Despite my flaws, I saw that God never left me, and I finally trusted he never would. Even when I doubted him or grew frustrated with him, he constantly loved me.

And so I learned I was not only surrounded by love, but worthy of love. True love. God's love.

TANGIBLE
THE STORY OF WILL
WRITTEN BY MARTY MINCHIN

Pachelbel's "Cannon in D" filled my tiny RV, and I settled onto the plaid couch to re-watch my wedding video — alone — for the hundredth time. My mom had given me a tiny TV/VCR combo for entertainment, and I watched as my high school sweetheart walked down the aisle.

I breathed deeply and closed my eyes, letting the good memories wash over me while taking a swig of beer. That beautiful teenage girl in the video was almost 30, and she was about to become my ex-wife.

How can I fix our marriage?

I cried big ugly tears that ran down my cheeks as I remembered what it felt like to have a wife and kids and a house.

No one depended on me anymore. I was the needy one, and the only one who took care of me was my estranged wife, Allison.

She brought our kids over to spend the weekend with me in the ratty old RV and usually dropped off some groceries. I could dumpster dive during the week, but I was glad to feed the kids real food.

The Ruger 9mm pistol I'd "borrowed" from my boss at the shop rested in my lap. I'd parked the RV on a hill overlooking the shop, and a weapon could be useful in case anyone tried to break in.

Right.

I picked up the gun and pressed the barrel to my temple. Then I cocked it and pulled the trigger.

Nothing happened.

I'm a veteran of the U.S. Marines. I know how to use weapons. That gun should not have jammed.

I rolled the gun back and forth in my hands, wondering if there was some bigger message. Clearly, my death was not meant to be, at least not that day.

The night was quiet as always, the tiny town long asleep. If I looked out the door of the RV, I could see a million stars in the sky.

The voice seemed to come from nowhere. I began crying, and my hands trembled so violently that the gun dropped to the floor.

Find MY truth, and you'll find yourself.

తతతత

Since I was a young teenager, my biggest dream in life was to be a family man. A lot of my high school friends were heading to the military or to college after graduation, and I just wanted to head to the altar. Allison and I met when we were 16 and working in the same car-detailing salon, and I couldn't wait to get married and start having kids. We got engaged while we were still in high school.

My job prospects after high school looked slim in

TANGIBLE

Rolla, Missouri. The town had fewer than 20,000 people, and the nearest big city, St. Louis, was almost two hours away by car. A career in the military seemed ideal. I could get out of town, explore the world and get paid for it. I checked out several branches, and I liked the tough, smart U.S. Marines.

As soon as I completed boot camp, I returned to Rolla to marry Allison in the small Methodist church I attended with my parents. My first assignment was to Okinawa, Japan, and Allison decided to stay home in the United States. The thought of living overseas was thrilling to me. I figured that a small town could only provide a snippet of life, and I longed to get out into the world and see what more it had to offer.

Japan was home to religions unfamiliar to me. I'd been baptized in the Methodist church a few months before, a symbolic act of being lowered into and raised out of a pool of water to represent that I believed in God and his son, Jesus. I didn't understand much about following God beyond that, and I was open to learning about the Eastern religions housed in the exotic shrines and temples of Okinawa. I tried Buddhism, Taoism and Shintoism, but the more I learned about them, the emptier I felt. The religions had the feel-good, spiritual element, but I couldn't find anything or anyone *tangible* at their core.

I lived in barracks in Okinawa with the other men and quickly noticed the manipulation that went on between the ranks. I missed Allison, and tension between us stretched across the ocean that separated us. Somehow rumors flew internationally that she was cheating, or I was cheating. That wasn't true for me, but I didn't know what was going on with my wife, so far away.

Allison agreed to come to Japan, and a friend from high school who was stationed in Okinawa with the U.S. Air Force agreed to let us stay in his apartment for her two-week visit.

I suspected that Allison and our friend had an affair while she was there. I never confronted her about it, and I never told her about the hostility that took root as a result of my suspicions. I tried to let the incident go, but over the years it always seemed to stick in my head, like a bat hanging in a cave that wouldn't fly away.

After my year in Asia, Allison and I reunited at a base in California. We moved around the state for three years, as I shifted between military jobs but never seemed to pick up rank. I felt like a number caught in a never-ending shuffle.

る。る。る。

The wind blew gently across Fallujah as my security team passed through the area. This small suburb of Bagdad had already been hit several times in the first phase of Operation Iraqi Freedom, and the chemicals from the attacks had settled into the sand, which was as fine as house dust and sat 18 inches deep over the bedrock underneath.

As we walked through the streets, our boots slapped

the hot pavement, and the sand swirled around our feet. The particles floated with the breeze and in with our breath. We exhaled the air, but a noxious mix of napalm, phosphorous and other chemical particles stayed in our lungs.

We felt nothing, but our lungs were about to get slaughtered by a thousand tiny knives.

ॐॐॐ

What is this?

I looked down at the tissue, which was spotted red and black.

Military doctors had me airlifted to Germany, where I coughed up so much black tarry substance that I almost choked to death. Seventeen of the 24 members of my security team had come down with the same bronchial disease.

The chemicals in the sand, which were then deposited in our lungs, had granulized and turned into shards. Every time we breathed in and out, they ripped through our lungs like sharp blades through tissue. After an endoscopy in Germany, nurses pulled a baby food jar full of shards out of my lungs.

A nurse dried a shard out, picked it up with tweezers and used it to cut a piece of paper in half.

"This is what happens every time you take a deep breath," she said.

I stared in disbelief.

EXPOSED

Doctors said the condition was serious and eventually fatal. They differed in their opinions, but no one said I'd live beyond my mid-30s. Every breath drove the shards deeper into my lung tissue.

I'd barely been in Iraq for two months. I flew home brimming with anger, self-judgment and depression. I had survived firefights and killed people. I'd gotten in a situation with my commander and seen an ugly side of military authority. I'd seen things that would haunt my dreams years later.

෭෭෭

I went to Iraq in February of 2003, and by June, Allison and I had moved into a house in Missouri. We had two children, and we tried to settle down.

I was angry, though. A fire built inside me in Iraq, and for years the smallest thing could set it to blaze like I'd added fresh kindling. If someone bumped into me in a store, I was ready to take out his whole family. Before Iraq, I ran at least three miles a day; after returning home, I couldn't walk from the kitchen to the living room without getting out of breath. I became a recluse and couldn't hold down a job because I could neither find the energy nor control my temper.

Ten years into our marriage, Allison met up again with the guy from Okinawa, but by that time there was little hope for saving our marriage. We were riding on a teeter-totter of a relationship, never willing to try to work it out at the same time. For two years, we took turns moving in and out of the house, separating and getting back together. In 2010, I moved out for good.

The problem was, I had nowhere to go.

Carl and I had met in a band after my return to Missouri. He played bass, and I played rhythm guitar, and he seemed pretty nice. He had a criminal record, but he'd served his time and was trying to clean up. Then in his 50s, Carl said he was too old to get down on his hands and knees and work on lawnmowers.

"You know, I've got a pretty good business going," he told me. "I'm looking for some help to keep up with the orders. With another set of hands, this could really take off."

"I have a pretty good job right now. I'm not really looking." For once, I had managed to find and keep steady work.

Carl pursed his lips. "Just think about it, okay? Opportunities like this don't come along very often. I'm set to pull in some big money, and you could get in on that."

I had to admit that I liked the sound of "big money," and if the business did flourish, I could really profit.

I decided to give it a shot.

For the first month, Carl and I worked 12-hour days, and the money and orders rolled in. He slept in the building's office and let me move a cot into the shop.

Those weeks, however, were like the worm on a fishhook. Once I bit, Carl had me. I was dependent on him for income and a place to stay. It wasn't long before he said he couldn't pay me as much.

While my income dried up, Carl's beer budget seemed to be flush. One of my daily duties became driving the four-wheeler down to the town's only restaurant and carting back huge cases of beer and liquor for Carl.

He drank a lot of his liquor stash at night while he watched boxing matches and old Westerns on YouTube. Sometimes he had women over. The more he drank, the angrier he became, and it became easier to stay away in the evenings.

I couldn't afford gas for my car, so instead I'd sit in it for hours or play my guitar outside the shop. Sometimes I walked to a nearby park and relaxed for a few hours until enough time had passed for Carl to fall asleep.

When Carl's friend dropped off an old RV, it looked like a mansion on wheels had rolled up. Squirrels had been living in it for several years and furnished it with acorns and grass. The interior stunk like turpentine and formaldehyde, and the roof leaked a small flood into the driver's seat when it rained. The RV technically was a gift to Carl, but he agreed that if I fixed it up, I could live in it.

I spent a few weeks removing the animal droppings and trying to make it livable. The drummer from the band worked on the electrical system, and I borrowed cleaning supplies from the shop to get rid of the stench. I used the little money I had to buy silicon to seal the leaks, and my mom bought me an inflatable mattress to sleep on. It didn't have heat or plumbing, but I could walk down the hill from the RV's parking place and use the shower and bathroom in the shop. I plugged an electric converter into the shop and got enough power to run my little TV, a few lights and a can opener.

Allison brought the kids out sometimes for the weekends so I could see them. Because I couldn't afford food, she had to leave enough groceries to feed them through the week, too. During the week, I begged people in town for food or stole out of the trash at the restaurant.

I lived in the RV for 10 months. I missed my family, and my nightly viewing of my wedding video only made me more depressed. When I took home Carl's gun, I truly felt like I had nothing to offer anyone and nothing to work toward. The future looked like a big black hole.

≈≈≈

The voice I heard that night would not be dismissed.

It echoed in my head that week, like Jiminy Cricket whispering in my ear. At first I stubbornly refused to acknowledge that perhaps God himself was speaking to me. But my life seemed to be enveloped by a thick gray cloud, and the voice reminded me that God could see through it.

Find MY truth, and you'll find yourself.

Maybe I should pay attention.

Okay, God. I finally relented. *I'll listen.*

≈≈≈

"Hey, Will. You wanna go to church with me on Sunday?"

I snapped my head up in shock. Carl's brother, who was a slightly more likable, less foul-mouthed drunk, was talking to me.

A shiver went down my spine that was so strong my shoulders vibrated.

"Uh, I don't know, Jake. I might have to do some work that morning."

"Okay." Jake shrugged his shoulders and walked out of the shop. I'd known him for almost a year, and he'd never mentioned church. The only time he came into the shop was to play guitar with Carl and me and down a bunch of beer. He and I had never really talked.

Jake wouldn't give up. He invited me to his church several more times that week. Each time, I hemmed and hawed an answer. Inside, though, I was starting to wonder. Why was he asking me so much?

What do you want, God? Is something bigger going on here?

I had to take Jake's request seriously. It seemed highly unlikely that he would have asked me to go to church so out of the blue on his own.

My kids stayed with me in the RV that weekend, and I dressed them up the best I could and took them to Jake's church. We settled into a pew in a room full of strangers.

The church service lasted two hours. I bawled like a baby for an hour and 45 minutes of it.

I had stepped into a whirlpool of self-realization. I

looked down at my kids, and my mind rushed back to the day I tried to kill myself in the RV. What had I been thinking? The two biggest reasons for me to live were sitting right next to me. I reached out and gently hugged them close as the tears began to fall.

The preacher seemed to be speaking right to me. He talked about how we all need to acknowledge the bad things we've done in the past. God, he said, forgives us of all of those things. When we believe in Jesus, ask him to be our friend and live our lives following him, we don't have to dwell on the past. We can have a *new beginning*, using our lives in a positive way. And that could start right now.

My list of wrongdoings seemed so long. When I'd lived with Allison and the kids, I spent most of the time locked in my music room. If the kids were getting on my nerves, I'd drive around for hours until long past their bedtime. I'd been angry and at times abusive to Allison. When I was in Iraq, I'd killed people.

How in the world can I turn all of that into a positive?

I cried harder, and my kids started crying with me. They didn't know what was going on, but they sensed the release of emotion, self-judgment and negativity that floated away from me like a giant helium balloon. I'm pretty sure they knew that their dad was actually happy.

I would live a new life, I decided, with God's help. I believed that God was real — I'd heard that voice speak and figured he must have prompted Jake's invitation to church. I was ready to start fresh, as a follower of God.

EXPOSED

૱૱૱

Several years before, my band had advertised on MySpace for a singer. I'd surfed around the site looking for musicians, and I came across Amy's profile.

She described herself as an "avid Christian" in her MySpace profile and said that she wasn't online for people to mess around with. She was a singer.

I sent her a message, and she replied that she was interested in auditioning for our band. She was attending college in St. Louis, and we could never find a time for a tryout that would work with all of our schedules. We kept in touch online, though. Sometime in the future, I thought, she could be good for the band.

Amy and I became social media friends. I could tell that she was sheltered and kept herself out of the social scene that many college students fell into. We messaged and texted for years, and she seemed kindhearted and understanding. She sent me uplifting messages, often with Bible verses attached. At first I didn't even read them, but on occasion I'd drag out the Bible I'd gotten at the Methodist church years before and look up the verse. Sometimes she'd write me messages about Jesus or ask me to pray.

It doesn't matter what God you believe in or if you believe at all. Just try Jesus, and see what comes from it.

I respected Amy and her choices in life, but I was still skeptical about God. How could I believe in something intangible? Plus, as a foul-mouthed Marine who spent a lot of time in bars, I could only take such positivity in small doses.

She persisted, and I slowly began to share my story with her. She listened to me, and then she would tell me she was sorry that was happening. "There's something out there for you," she'd say. "You could pray, or I could pray for you."

A day or two before I'd tried to commit suicide, Amy had texted me, out of the blue.

I haven't heard from you for a few years. I just thought I would say hi. I hope you're still alive. If you are, here's a Bible verse.

I ran into Amy a few days after I had attended Jake's church.

"If you want, you can come to church with my family," she said. "We've gone to Christian Life Center for a long time, and it's a great place."

"Sure."

She smiled, looking both pleased and surprised. I knew I needed to go to church if I wanted to follow God, and I liked Amy and her parents, who I'd gotten to know a little about through her messages.

ॐॐॐ

Amy's mom and dad were filled with insight and good advice. As I got more involved in their church, her parents became mentors, and the church congregation became my family. They encouraged me to read the Bible, and they helped me understand it. I began to grasp what it looked like to follow God, and I trusted Amy and her parents to help me think through the many problems that remained unresolved in my life.

The biggest issue was Allison, who was still my wife.

"How are things going with her?" Amy's dad asked.

"I really want to try to make things work." I believed that God didn't want us to have broken relationships in our lives, and I was willing to try to put my marriage back together.

Amy's parents suggested I try *The Love Dare*, a 40-day Christian marriage program where you read a Bible passage every day and do something for your spouse to try and create or recreate a loving marriage.

I was willing to try, and Allison agreed to let me move out of the RV and into our house. We both had been seeing other people, and we agreed to put those relationships on hold for 40 days.

"Allison, I've been going to church, and I want to give this a shot." She seemed open to it. "I'm trying to work on myself, and I'm willing to do my part if you'll do yours."

I showed her *The Love Dare* book, and she nodded a lot while I explained it to her, but she didn't say much.

"Okay, yes, I'll try it." Her voice didn't carry much enthusiasm, but I was heartened that she was at least willing to try.

I worked hard for 40 days. Each morning, the book laid out a task. The first ones were easy, like setting out a bowl of cereal, a spoon and a cup of milk for Allison before she got up.

TANGIBLE

She seemed underwhelmed by the gestures.

As the days went on, the tasks became more involved.

One night, I wrote down five positive things about Allison. I asked her to do the same, and we'd talk about our lists the next day.

I poured my heart into my list, thinking hard about the years I'd known Allison and why I'd fallen in love with her back in high school. We traded lists in the morning.

I gave her 10 handwritten pages. It looked like she'd put about five seconds of thought into her list.

1. You're a good dad.
2. You're a good cook.

Around day 23, I wrote Allison a note that was not required by the book. I explained that I wasn't trying to manipulate her and that I was following *The Love Dare* to the letter. I left a copy of the book on the kitchen table in hopes that she would read it. Like many of the gestures I'd made, it went unacknowledged.

I completed — or attempted to complete — all 40 tasks in the book. On day 43, I sat in shock as I realized I'd put in a month and a half of work and hadn't made a dent. We were over.

The old anger bubbled up, but I gave it a few days before I discussed the failed experiment with Allison.

"I meant what I said," she told me, resting her hand on my arm. "I'm not mad, but I'm done. I think you know that we both need to move on."

EXPOSED

She went back to the guy she'd been seeing before *The Love Dare* and packed to move out of town. After years of discord, we officially legally separated.

෩෩෩

I stayed in the house, but I couldn't keep up with the mortgage and soon faced foreclosure proceedings. Amy's parents, who had been advising me throughout that time, encouraged me to stay positive. When *The Love Dare* experiment fell apart, they saw that I had put in my time trying to make it work. To help me financially, they invited me to live in their home for a year.

I pulled my weight by cutting wood and cleaning around the house. Amy, who had moved home after graduating from college while she looked for a job, became a close friend. Her family became my friends and my family. They let my kids stay with me at the house on the weekends, and during the week, Amy and I often hung out at the Baptist Student Union on the local college campus. We played board games and went to potluck dinners. We cooked meals together and had pizza nights with our friends. I spent many Friday evenings watching movies with Amy and her parents.

I read the Bible every night, and when I had questions, Amy or her parents would help me. I was learning more about God, and I was watching a Christian family operate with an insider's view. I wanted a life like theirs.

TANGIBLE

༈ ༈ ༈

I opened the door to my new apartment and took a deep breath. Other than my 10 months in the RV, I'd never lived independently. My stomach fluttered as I walked inside. I felt like a 19-year-old kid who had just moved out of his parents' house.

Could I do this on my own without Amy and her family to keep me in line and focused on God?

I'd started drinking when I was 11 years old, and I knew my tendency to get into trouble. I wanted to stay on the path I'd walked with Amy's family, living a life getting to know God.

Thanks to my connections at Christian Life Center, I'd learned about a job opening. The brothers who owned it, all Christians, hired me and soon treated me like another sibling. We started out with workspace in a basement and a barn and grew into a multi-million-dollar company with a 6,500-square-foot building.

My friendship with Amy had been going strong for years, and even though she was younger than me, I saw her as a mentor. She had pulled me out of the fire during some dark days with her prayers and encouragement. The years of Bible verses and kind messages had impacted my life, and she had taught me what it looked like to make God the first priority in my life.

Amy and I had joined a small group of people from our church who got together regularly to eat a meal, study the Bible and talk. Years before, I would have been the sullen jarhead in the corner looking at his shoes and unwilling to talk much to people I didn't know. I've told people that, before, you had to be a member of my family or know me for at least a decade before I'd crack a joke. But I started laughing and joking all of the time. I became open to listening to people, learning their stories and getting to know them.

Through it all, Amy has been my rock. She found me in a pile of ashes and helped me grow into a calm and caring person. She helped me get to know God better, and she's been a friend I knew would always support me.

She became someone I could fall in love with. And I did. One Thanksgiving Day, she became my girlfriend.

చళళళ

"Amy, did you see what we built out behind the house this weekend?" Amy's dad was playing his part perfectly.

"No, what is it?"

I smiled and stuffed my hand in my pocket to check on the ring one more time. "Come on, I'll show you."

I grabbed Amy's hand and led her outside toward an arbor I'd built beside her parents' barn. As we walked down the path, her dad plugged in the lights I'd wrapped around the wooden arch.

Amy looked at me quizzically. My mom and aunt and Amy's sister — who had flown in from out of state — joined us.

As they hugged, I dropped to one knee and waited for Amy to turn around. My eyes were already tearing up.

TANGIBLE

I had chosen a quote from Amy's favorite chick flick, *The Notebook*.

"The best love is the kind that awakens the soul and makes us reach for more, that plants a fire in our hearts and brings peace to our minds. And that's what you've given me. That's what I'd hoped to give you forever ... cause if you're a bird, I'm a bird."

I couldn't stop grinning.

"Amy, will you marry me?"

She said yes.

We celebrated for the entire weekend. We ate dinner together, sat around a bonfire, drank wine and told stories with all of our friends and family.

We continued to grow every day as we prayed together and talked to God about what he wanted for our lives and our future home. We were ready to spend the rest of our lives together — each of us and God.

CONCLUSION

Our mission at Christian Life Center is to share fresh hope in real and relevant ways. No matter where they've been, who has hurt them or who they have hurt, we want to encourage everyday people right where they are, to show them light can shine into the dark, lonely places. Life can get good — really good!

We want to shock people who think they know what church looks like by showing them Jesus in some unconventional ways. We want people who believe no one will accept them to know *we will* support them. We want people to know they are forgivable, to know that God sees them and loves what he sees.

We believe you read this book because God brought it to you, seeking to reveal his love to you on a personal level. We have prayed you would come to know that you are not alone. Whether you're a man or a woman, a logger or a waitress, blue collar or no collar, a parent or a student, have a college degree or are a graduate of the school of hard knocks, we believe God came to save you. He came to save all of us from the hellish pain we've wallowed in and offer lasting joy and the opportunity to share in real life, available forever through faith in Jesus Christ.

Do you have honest questions that such radical change is possible? It seems too good to be true, doesn't it? Each of us at CLC warmly invites you to come and check out our Christian Life Center family. Freely ask questions, examine our statements, see if we're "for real" and, if you choose, journey with us at whatever pace you are comfortable. You will find that we are far from perfect.

Our scars and sometimes open wounds are still healing. We want you to know God is still completing the process of authentic life change in us. We still make mistakes in our journey, like everyone will. Therefore, we acknowledge our continued need for each other's forgiveness and support. We need the love of God just as much as we did the day before we believed in him.

If you are unable to be with us, yet you sense you would really like to experience such a life change, here are some basic thoughts to consider. If you choose, at the end of reading this, you can pray the suggested prayer. If your prayer genuinely comes from your heart, you will experience the beginning stages of authentic life change, similar to those you have read about.

How does this change occur?

Recognize that what you're doing isn't working. Accept the fact that Jesus desires to forgive you for your bad decisions and selfish motives. Realize that without this forgiveness, you will continue a life separated from God and his amazing love. In the Bible, the book of Romans, chapter 6, verse 23 tells us that the result of sin (seeking our way rather than God's way) is death, but the gift that God freely gives is everlasting life found in Jesus Christ.

CONCLUSION

Believe in your heart that God passionately loves you and wants to give you a new life.

Believe in your heart that, "if you confess with your mouth that Jesus is Lord and believe in your heart that God raised him from the dead, you will be saved" (Romans 10:9 NLT).

Believe in your heart that because Jesus paid for your mistakes and wrong motives, and because you asked him to forgive you, he has filled your new heart with his life in such a way that he transforms you from the inside out. Second Corinthians 5:17 reads, "When someone becomes a Christian, he becomes a brand new person inside. He is not the same anymore. A new life has begun!"

Why not pray now?

Lord Jesus, my choices have not resulted in the happiness I hoped they would bring. If I've learned one thing in my journey, it's that you are God and I am not. Not only have I experienced pain, I've also caused it. I know I am separated from you, but I want that to change. I am sorry for the choices I've made that have hurt myself and others and denied you. I believe your death paid for my sins, and you are now alive to transform me from the inside out. Would you please do that now? I ask you to come and live in me so that I can sense you are here with me. Thank you for hearing and changing me. Now please help me know when you are speaking to me, so I can choose the life you want me to have and become the person you meant me to be. Amen.

The Show-Me State's unfolding story of God's love is still being written — and your name is in it. Let Jesus show you the beautiful new chapter he's ready to write with you. We hope to see you this Sunday!

Eddie and Karen Jones
CLC Pastors
Rolla, Missouri

We would love for you to join us at Christian Life Center!

We meet Sunday mornings at 9:45 and 11:15 a.m. at 305 East 1ˢᵗ Street, Rolla, MO 65401.

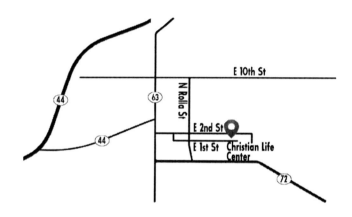

Contact Information
Phone: 573.364.2026
Web site: www.clcrolla.com
Email: info@clcrolla.com
Facebook: www.facebook.com/clcrolla

Mailing Address
P.O. Box 1567
Rolla, MO 65402

For more information on reaching your city with
stories from your church, go to
www.testimonybooks.com.

GOOD CATCH
PUBLISHING